UNDERCURRENTS

Richard Skinner is a writer working across fiction, life writing, essays, non-fiction and poetry. He has published three novels with Faber and two previous collections of essays, *Vade Mecum* (Zer0 Books, 2015) and *Joiners* (Vanguard Editions, 2019). He has also had published eight books of poems. He is Director of the Fiction Programme at Faber Academy and is currently studying mysticism at Sarum Theological College.

Also by Richard Skinner

FICTION

The Red Dancer	(Faber & Faber reissue, 2017)
The Mirror & The Velvet Gentleman	(Faber & Faber, 2014)

NON-FICTION

Joiners	(Vanguard Editions, 2019)
Writing a Novel	(Faber & Faber, 2018)
The Busby Babes	(Urbane Publications, 2016)
Vade Mecum: Essays, Reviews & Interviews	(Zer0 Books, 2015)
Dub: Red Hot vs Ice Cold	(NOCH, 2013)

POETRY

White Noise Machine	(Salt, 2023)
Dream into Play	(Poetry Saltzburg, 2022)
Invisible Sun	(Smokestack, 2021)
The Malvern Aviator	(Smokestack, 2018)
Terrace	(Smokestack, 2015)
the light user scheme	(Smokestack, 2013)

CONTENTS

BOOKS

FILMS

MUSIC

LIFE WRITING

INTERVIEWS

Undercurrents

Richard Skinner

Broken Sleep Books

ISBN: 978-1-917617-22-2

Cover designed by Aaron Kent

Cover art: © KurArt / Adobe Stock

Edited and Typeset by Aaron Kent

Broken Sleep Books Ltd
PO BOX 102
Llandysul
SA44 9BG

I believe that the highest achievement of a novelist is the ability to construct the form of a novel as an enigma – a puzzle whose solution reveals the novel's centre.
— Orhan Pamuk

THE NARRATIVE TRIANGLE

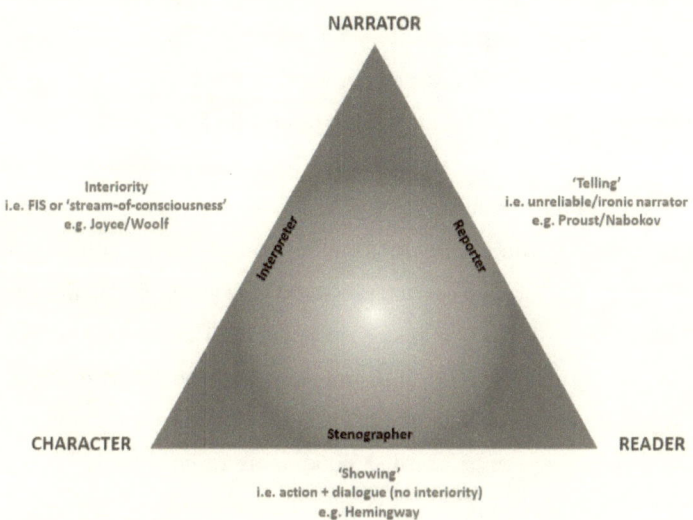

IN every text, there is a set of three relationships – that between the narrator and character, between character and the reader, and between the reader and the narrator. According to whichever one of those three relationships you wish to highlight, you will have to use your narrator in different ways and to different degrees.

So, if you want the closest possible relationship between character and your reader, you will have to use your narrator like a stenographer – someone present in the story-world whose sole job is to relay to the reader what the characters say and do. The narrator-as-stenographer has no voice of their own, they offer no opinions or value judgements on any of those words or actions, they are just silent recorders.

The early short stories by Hemingway that feature a character called Nick Adams are a good example of this kind of role for the narrator. In story after story, we see Nick Adams go hunting, or fishing, putting up a tent and taking it down the next morning. We are offered no commentary on any of this by the narrator – the stories are pure transcripts of word and action. If we want to know what Nick Adams is thinking or how he feels, we will have to infer it for ourselves purely from what Nick Adams says and does. In this type of narration, we have direct, first-hand access to what the characters say and do. There is no 'interiority'. This is 'showing' at its purest – so stripped down and without any narratorial comment, Hemingway's early stories could almost read like a film scripts. Dashiel Hammet's stories and novels are another good example. Acting purely as a pane of glass, the narrator-as-stenographer is nowhere to be seen or heard. A good, more recent example of this style of narration is John William's fine novel *Stoner*.

At some point, however, the narrator may pierce the body of a character and enter their hearts and minds, revealing to the reader what the character is feeling and thinking. This could be done only occasionally, and very briefly, via 'free indirect style', those moments when the narrator climbs inside the head of a character and allows us to hear what they are thinking. Take this extract from Virginia Woolf's *Mrs Dalloway*:

> He dropped her hand. Their marriage was over, he thought, with agony, with relief. The rope was cut; he mounted; he was free, as it was decreed that he, Septimus, the lord of men, should be free, alone (since his wife had thrown away her wedding ring; since she had left him), he, Septimus, was alone, called forth in advance of the mass of men to hear the truth, to learn the meaning, which now at last, after all the toils of civilization – Greeks, Romans, Shakespeare, Darwin, and now himself – was to be given whole to… "To whom?" he asked aloud.

After the complete action – 'He dropped her hand' – comes a bit of reported speech: 'Their marriage was over, he thought, with agony, with relief.' We know this is reported speech because of the tag 'he thought' – the narrator here is 'telling' us what Septimus thinks. What follows, however, is a chain of thoughts that we have access to without the narrator 'telling' us via a tag that the character is thinking. It is the thoughts themselves that we are hearing, that the narrator allows us to hear, without offering any judgement or opinion themselves on those thoughts. This act of listening-in on Septimus' thoughts is ended when he speaks aloud. This is free indirect style. It is still reported, of course, and therefore 'indirect' in that the narrator is relaying those thoughts to us, but there are no tags, hence the 'free' in free indirect style.

The area that separates free indirect style from 'telling' is very grey. What free indirect style is for some people is the narrator telling us something for others. So how can we know the difference? Fortunately, there is a litmus test: whenever you think you've spotted a moment of free indirect style, say it out loud to yourself. Does it sound like the kind of thing a person would naturally say to themselves? (The key word here is 'naturally'.) If so, then it is free indirect style. If not, then it is the narrator telling us something. If the spoken-out-loud sentence sounds a bit stiff, it is not the kind of thing a person would naturally think to themselves, and so it is not free indirect style. Moments of free indirect style tend to be colloquial – usually swearing, or characters asking themselves questions – so the more colloquial it sounds, the more likely it is free indirect style.

Free indirect style is best summed up as a fusion of third-person narration with first-person consciousness. It can only exist in third-person narration because, by its very definition, we are always inside the head of a character in first-person narration. Free indirect style is best used sparingly, just moments sprinkled here and there throughout the writing. It is an amazing way to reveal character, it brings them alive for the reader. If free indirect style is used over a longer period of time, for a whole paragraph, or perhaps a few pages, it becomes something else – interior monologue. If the narrator moves furthest inside the mind and body of the character, narration becomes something else again – stream-of-consciousness, which captures not only the product of thought but the thought process itself. Stream-of-consciousness is body language, but without the body.

In all these forms of narration – free indirect style, interior monologue and stream-of-consciousness, the role of the narrator is as an interpreter, sitting in a booth with headphones on, just listening to what a character is thinking to themselves and delivering those thoughts as accurately as possible without any comment or value judgement of their own. This is the narrator-as-interpreter. Both roles – narrator-as-stenographer and narrator-as-interpreter – have in common the fact that the narrators offer either just the character's words and actions, or access to their hearts and minds, without expressing any opinion or passing any judgement on those things. If, however, the narrator starts to offer opinion, comments or value judgements on what is happening in the story or on what the characters are thinking and feeling, then another role comes into play: the narrator-as-reporter.

In this role, not only is the narrator telling a story, whether it be their own story in first-person narration or someone else's in third-person narration, but they are also offering us their opinions or value judgements on those stories. And, when they offer those opinions or value judgements, they are talking directly to us, the reader. In the most extreme forms of this kind of narration, direct access to the words and actions of the characters can get lost all together. Perhaps the best example of this extremity is Proust, in which his characters' words and actions get lost in the mists and maze of time and receding memory. In his essay on Proust, Nabokov said, 'Proust's fundamental ideas regarding the flow of time concern the constant evolution of personality in terms of duration, the unsuspected riches of our subliminal minds which we can retrieve only by an act of intuition, of memory, of involuntary associations.' We could not be further removed from character and action here.

This mode of narrator-as-reporter is all about how the personality of the narrator is revealed to us via the narrator's 'voice'. It offers an added layer of narration on top of the story, a layer through which everything is refracted, coloured, like a filter on a camera. This allows narrators room for manoeuvre when telling their own story. They may be unreliable about what they are telling us, or they may adopt an ironic tone towards the story of their life. Humbert Humbert in Nabokov's novel *Lolita* is the perfect example of a narrator who adopts unreliability and irony in order to shade, slant or skewer the truth from us.

It is interesting to think that Proust and Hemingway were living and writing in the same city at the same time. I can't think of two writers more different. For me, they are the north and south poles of writing in terms of their prose styles and the roles they gave their narrator – Hemingway writes in simple declarative sentences and his stories deal in discrete moments, usually through action and dialogue; Proust, on the other hand, writes endlessly long, digressive sentences, full of sub-clauses and his novel encompasses generations, time itself. Marcel as narrator is mainly interested in interiority and description. As writers, we have to find our place on the spectrum between these two poles.

And all of us as writers have to find our place within this triangle, depending on what kind of role you assign to your narrator and, consequently, which relationship in your writing you wish to promote the most. If you want the reader to be left alone to infer directly from the words and actions of your characters what those characters think and feel, then you will be working along the base of the triangle with your narrator acting as a stenographer. If, however, you want the reader to have access to the deep recesses of your character's mind and the dark chambers of their heart, you will be moving along the left edge of the triangle with your narrator adopting the role of interpreter. Finally, if you wish your narrator to address the reader directly, not only telling us what happened but also offering up their opinions and judgements, then you will be working along the right-hand side of the triangle, where the narrator is acting as a reporter. We writers all sit somewhere inside this triangle – pinpoint where you think you sit and mark a dot there.

PROUST'S 'CROSS-HATCHING OF INSTANTS'

The psychic absorbs the cosmic and Being itself is diluted in style.

... metonymy is the means of establishing the Proustian analogy in space.

*... analogy['s]... sealed 'links', its cross-hatching of instants, become
deployed within [by?] the action of the novel...*
— Julia Kristeva

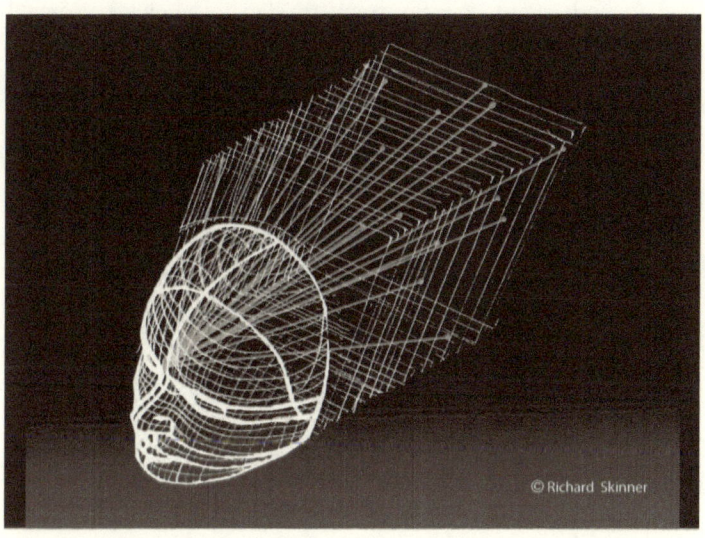

© Richard Skinner

WHEN I read these quotes from Julia Kristeva's book on Proust entitled *Proust and the Sense of Time*, I imagined that, as we live and the passage of time flows, so we are constantly experiencing things, mostly without our realising it. These can be cognitive processes, like thinking to yourself, 'I must get milk and bread', but also perceptions. So, for example, while walking along a path, it would be perfectly normal to say to yourself 'I must get milk and bread' but it would be rare to say to yourself 'That rose is red' when you pass a garden. The former is a verbalised thought, whereas the latter is something perceived. The former is actively sought whereas the latter is something 'felt' rather than verbalised, something that comes to you unbidden. Thanks to MRI scanning, scientists have now given a name to these 'felt' moments, these moments of sensual perception, and the word is 'qualia'.

In the early days of MRI scanning (mid '90s), I volunteered to take part in a research programme that was looking at how stroke victims could relearn speech. In order to know how to do that, they had to understand how the brain reacted to language. When I volunteered, I was injected with a barium solution, strapped into a kind of stretcher and then inserted into an MRI scanner, where I stayed for several hours. It was a very weird experience! I felt like an astronaut. I was wearing headphones and there was a constant flow of words. I didn't have to do anything in response. Afterwards, they showed me the coloured scans of my brain as it was listening the the stream of words. The scans looked like firework displays in thick fog. They explained to me that every word I heard caused synapses in my brain to fire off, and these firings were caught by the magnetic properties of the barium that was flowing through my system. They realised that the brain reacts to every single thing it perceives, and every single one of these perceptions is called a 'qualia'. Brilliant.

So, back to Proust: I imagined that we are experiencing these instances of qualia all the time, without our knowing, and these moments are constantly receding as time passes. In the image, these moments are the red dots on the square planes, each of which (the planes, I mean) represents a minute, say. There are 20 planes, so 20 minutes. So, behind us, flowing away from us all the time are these instances of perception, and they stretch forever backwards. In Proust's book, the famous dipping of the scallop-shell-shaped anamnestic madeleine into the tea is a moment when this *action* precipitates an involuntary memory of a moment years earlier, a moment that comes to him unbidden. In that exact moment in time, past and present are fused into a moment of transcendence and the narrator is suddenly sent back in time. In the image, these moments of fusion are the red lines connecting the qualia (red dot) to our minds. But, of course, we're not 'sent' back in time, it is the past moment that comes zipping forward to us. So, the direction of travel on those red lines is from the red dot to the brain, not the other way round. Those past planes of consciousness are collapsed into now by the involuntary memory, and it is that collapsing that fuses past and present and allows us a moment of transcendence outside the flow of time. Indeed, I imagine that those red lines are actually elastic, constantly twitching with qualia and pulling back and forth, thus constantly moving those planes of consciousness backwards and forwards, like shuffling a deck of cards. I think this is how memory works; that memory is largely an unbidden process, but is happening all the time. These memories constitute our Being, they make us who we are – where would we be without our memories? This is what is so distressing about memory loss via amnesia or dementia, both of which rob us of our memory.

On a side note, I sometimes used to go to the free lunchtime lectures held in Holborn and Susan Greenfield once gave a fascinating lecture on amnesia and dementia. She defined 'explicit memory' as to do with events and facts, whereas 'implicit memory' is to do with skills and habits. Amnesiacs, she said, suffer defects in explicit memories; but implicit memories are preserved because they rely on 'sensory motor coordination'. Amnesia is a confusion of time and place, not self. However, patients suffering from Parkinson's and Huntingdon's diseases have no problem remembering facts and events. Dementia is a confusion of self, not time and place. Amnesiacs lose their identity, whereas dementia patients lose their independence.

So, the image is my attempt at visualising what I understand Proust to mean when he suggests that we may travel in time via the process of involuntary memory.

ONE HUNDRED YEARS OF SOLITUDE
BY GABRIEL GARCÍA MÁRQUEZ

The tone that I eventually used in One Hundred Years of Solitude *was based on the way my grandmother used to tell stories. She told things that sounded supernatural and fantastic, but she told them with complete naturalness.*
– Gabriel García Márquez

IT took me four days solid to read this, so transfixed was I. What a book! As Milan Kundera says, 'García Márquez's novel is free imagination itself. One of the greatest works of poetry I know. Every single sentence sparkles with fantasy, every sentence is a surprise, is wonder.' One of the hardest things about the book is keeping track of who's who – there's a lot of slippage. Children are constantly born in and out of wedlock and everyone is somehow related to everyone else. It's a story of contrasts, crossovers and worlds collapsing into each other – living/dead, inside/outside, past/present, rural/urban, knowledge/ignorance, democracy/totalitarianism. Every event carries equal weight and significance – a life is summarised in a few lines, someone's death is mentioned only in passing, and then the narrative quickly moves on to a much more detailed description of how a house is built. Although the narrative is written as one long monologue, without 'scenes', it's a very 'readerly' book, in that it invites many and various interpretations (my good friend Jason Watkins wrote a paper on it when we were at uni – he got a first) and I can see why – it is so rich in themes/motifs/imagery (the yellow butterflies!). As another friend, Alex, pointed out, it's also a time-travel book. The similarly-named characters are perpetually born and face the same hardships, prejudices and grudges in their lives, so we get a sense of permanent *déjà-vu*. All the women either die young or live well into old age under a vow of silence and all the men are shot. Such repetition halts the progress of time; time is cyclical, we cover 100 years and yet it goes by – poof – just like that... Like all great novels, it immerses you in its world and shows you how life is. There isn't another book like it in the whole of the world. It stands tall, blocking out the light and casting a huge shadow. Majestic.

HOPSCOTCH BY JULIO CORTÁZAR

JULIO Cortázar's postmodernist novel *Hopscotch* is a novel of forking paths. On the one hand, you can read chapters 1-56 in order. That way, we follow the story of Horacio Oliveira, an Argentine intellectual slumming it in 1960s Paris. Oliveira is in love with a woman called Lucía, whom he calls 'La Maga' ('The Magician'). We follow their life in Paris. There is a mix of conventional dialogue/action scenes with non-narrative discourse. He, La Maga and their group of bohemian friends from (among other places) Herzegovina and Montevideo hang out in bars and bedrooms, playing jazz records and squabbling existentially with each other. Nothing much happens. And yet everything. The mundanity of everyday life is raised to the level of the sublime and vice versa. So far, so good.

On the other hand, before the novel starts, Cortázar inserts a suggestion to the reader that they should read the novel haphazardly. He issues a 'table of instructions' that requires the reader to hop from chapter to chapter, seemingly without connection. This way, reading the novel is like watching a film whose scenes are edited in the wrong order. When I say 'wrong', I am wrong, of course. There is no 'right' or 'wrong' way to order events. Conventional narrative observes the laws of cause and effect but this sequence places 'consecutiveness' above causality. Things happen in spite of, not because of, what has happened before.

Cortázar's suggestion means that causality becomes a casualty. Set this way, scenes are placed in harsh juxtaposition. Jolted out of our expectations, we lurch from scene to scene, fumbling to make a connection where there is seemingly none.

At first, this is bewildering, but at some point, this bewilderment becomes exhilaration. At the end of each section, we have no idea what will happen next. Time and again, we are pulled back to zero. Now, we are walking through the story, not in a straight line, but in Brownian motion. And isn't that a more natural way to experience a place and time? Nature is chaos, not order. We put events into an order so as to understand them – plot them into a story – but life itself is haphazard, isn't it?

Hopscotch is a random amble through the city. Because there's no linear narrative flow, you can dip in and out of the book, never knowing how close or far away you are from the end. An aimless walk, a wander without purpose. It takes time to adjust, but once accepted, it becomes addictive. Cortázar's interest in the layout of Paris bears similarities with Walter Benjamin's *Arcades Project* and André Breton's novel *Nadja*: 'Paris is a centre, you understand, a mandala through which one must pass without dialectics, a labyrinth where pragmatic formulas are of no use except to get lost in.'

Published in Buenos Aires in 1963 (and in English in 1966), Cortázar's novel was written at the height of the postmodern project (interestingly, its aleatory technique was adopted at the same time by composer John Cage, who used the I Ching to compose many of his pieces). His fellow Latin American authors quickly recognised Cortázar's achievement and his novel is now regarded, along with Márquez's *One Hundred Years of Solitude*, as the greatest novel published in the Spanish language since *Don Quixote*. His successor is fellow *enfant terrible* Roberto Bolaño, whose mammoth (and astonishing) novel *2666* (2004) might be read as a homage to Cortázar. Although now more than 60 years old, the play and freedom found in *Hopscotch*, its sense of dislocation and displaced identities, seem astoundingly current. Over those years, *Hopscotch* has not lost its zest for life one jot.

THE HOUSE OF LIFE BY MARIO PRAZ

IF this book didn't exist, it wouldn't be missed. It refers to nothing other than itself. It is of no use to anyone except the author. It doesn't present an argument, or defend a cause. It pursues no line of enquiry; it claims no new area of research. And yet, it contains multitudes and expands horizons. It is a world unto itself and obeys its own laws. Forgoing any sense of causality or flow, the book instead uses the *objets d'art* and sculptures, walls hung with paintings and prints, bureaus overflowing with postcards and ephemera in the author's opulent Roman apartment as sites for infinite meditation, as points from which to dive into the dark recesses of the author's life and memory. A bust reminds him of a long-ago trip to Chatsworth House, which in turn brings back the memory of a certain young lady. In this way, the work presents memory after memory, moving sideways, or scattershot, the way memory does without rhyme or reason. This procession is mirrored and echoed in the layout of the apartment, with its secret passages, false facades and blocked-up doors. Memory-houses as mazes. This *wunderkammer* of a book predates the work of WG Sebald by 30 years but I feel certain Sebald must have known about it as his work shares Praz's nostalgic, elegiac tone. I was influenced by Sebald when I wrote my debut novel, *The Red Dancer*, in which I included many non-fiction chapters that arrested and opened up the narrative with highly-detailed description. And so, without being aware of its existence, I was also influenced by *The House of Life*. A book of endless depth and beauty (it's also very funny).

THE MIRROR – A CASE STUDY

Every mirror is false because it repeats something it has not witnessed.
— Chazal

In 2004, I read a book called *Virgins of Venice* by Professor Mary Laven, a study of the enclosed lives of nuns in Renaissance Venice. Based on scrupulously researched material, the book presents astonishingly fresh and immediate insights into the reality of day-to-day life inside these convents. In the 16th century, convents weren't just spiritual institutions, they were also dumping grounds for orphans, illegitimate girls and the 'unmarriageable' women of Venetian noble families and so, while some of the nuns were cloistered by choice, others were not. This led to friction as some of the nuns who were dumped into convents sought the kind of existence that was at odds with conventual life. I was immediately drawn to the themes in the book and started to imagine what life must have been like for a young woman forced to enter a cloistered life. What would her life be like? How on earth would she cope? What thoughts would run through her mind? I started making notes and, without realising it, I had started planning a novel.

One of the main things that preoccupied me from the outset was the setting – a convent in Venice. How would I deal with that? Obviously, I read and researched extensively around that subject, but two things happened that were key. The first of these was that I travelled to Venice to see a convent for myself. Venice in the 16th century was home to more than 50 convents and, although there is a similar number today, there are only a handful of those original nunneries that have retained their function into the 21st century. One of these is Sant'Alvise, founded in 1388 as a hermitage for Augustinian nuns. Sant'Alvise lies in Cannaregio, one of the six historic *sestieri* of Venice and the northernmost of the city. This area of Venice was once solitary and remote and Sant'Alvise is situated on its northernmost edge. Nothing lies north of Sant'Alvise except the lagoon. This appealed to me and I decided to use Sant'Alvise as my model.

In June 2009, I travelled to Venice to see if I could gain entrance to the convent to see the interior for myself. I lived in Italy for two years in my early twenties and can get by in Italian, but I had prepared a little speech explaining who I was and what I wanted. On my first day, I walked to Sant'Alvise and stood outside. The simple façade of the convent is bare brick – plain, unassuming. No passerby would ever have known that it was a convent. I knocked on the middle door of the three. I was nervous. After a few moments, the door was opened by a small nun. I recited my prepared speech and asked for permission to enter the convent. The nun listened kindly and, when I had finished, told me that the Mother Superior was out and that I should come back in an hour. The door closed. I was crushed. I sat on the bridge and waited. Eventually I saw another, very small nun carrying shopping bags enter the convent by the door. I waited a few minutes, then knocked again. The same nun as before answered and nodded to me to wait. The nun who had been carrying the bags came to the door and I realised that she must be the Mother Superior. I recited my speech again and asked for permission to enter the convent. The Mother Superior also listened kindly and, when I had finished, replied 'Non.' She smiled and closed the door. That was that.

To console myself, I went into the church that is connected to the convent. Inside, it was very dark. The church was empty. On entering, you are immediately overshadowed by the wood-beamed underside of the nun's choir gallery (known as a *barco*), raised 3-4 metres off the ground by two wooden columns. Connected to the adjacent convent via a 'bridge', this choir gallery is where the nuns would come several times a day and night to hear mass and hold their own services out of sight of the public. The front of this choir gallery was a bare brick wall, about 6-7 metres high, punctuated by seven curtained grilles, enabling the invisible nuns to hear and be heard. Above the fourth grille was an oculus, a peep-hole onto the congregation below. All this detail was a gold mine for me and would feature prominently in the novel.

I spent a long time in there, taking notes and drawing diagrams and, just as I was leaving, I spotted in the gloom some small paintings on the wall. They were at head height and, as I drew nearer, I saw that they were panels, not paintings. There were eight of them, each depicting a scene from the Bible. The figures in them were simply painted and the flat perspective was not at all correct. Some of the figures in the back ground were bigger than those in the foreground. The colours were muted – brown, ochre, dark green, with some red in the pantaloons, robes and a parasol. I found out later that these panels are attributed to Lazzaro Bastiani and were painted some time in the late 15th century. They are the only work extant by Bastiani. On my way out, I saw that there were postcards of these panels on sale. I dropped my coins in the box and took two – "The Finding of Joseph" and "Joshua Taking Jericho". Again, these postcards were to prove precious and details from them appear in the novel.

At around the same time, the other thing that happened was that a friend of mine who worked in the Courtauld Library rang me one day. 'You'll never guess what I've just found,' he said. 'What?' I replied. He went on to tell me that the Courtauld just happened to have in their library sets of architectural plans for dozens of convents in Venice during the Renaissance, including

Sant'Alvise. What are the odds? How on earth did the plans end up there? I couldn't believe my luck. I took it as a sign that I was on the right track. I spent days in the library pouring over the plans for Sant'Alvise, building the convent brick by brick in my head. By the time I had finished, I knew every square inch of the interior of Sant'Alvise. I knew how many steps it was from the front door to the well, from the well to the kitchen. I knew how many steps there were up to the choir. I knew how big the orchard was.

With my fictional world built so surely in my head, I was now free to let my mind turn its attention to the story. During my research, I discovered that the manufacture of mirrors in the glass factories on Murano was well underway by the 15th century, which is also when the science of perspective entered Western painting. These two events are symbiotically linked. Before the Florentine architect and engineer Filippo Brunelleschi (1377-1446) began developing the rules of perspective in the early 15th century, most art was depicted on a flat plane, with characters and objects sized according to their spiritual or thematic significance. By painting the outlines of various Florentine buildings onto a mirror, Brunelleschi noted that when a building's outline was continued, all the lines converged on the horizon. In 1436, the mathematician and art theorist Leon Battista Alberti published his treatise on painting, *Della Pittura*. His and Brunelleschi's work created a fervent obsession with perspective among Italian artists who used the new science to full effect. For many, however, perspective was the original sin of Western painting because it was the first step in art's gradual succumbing to the outside world, to the exterior, at the expense of the spiritual, the interior.

So, one of my main characters would be a painter who uses a mirror in his painting, and the moment he brings a mirror into the convent would be the inciting incident. The mirror is seen as diabolical by the nuns and all hell breaks loose the moment the painter brings it into the convent. There is a line in the movie *The Draughtsman's Contract* that has always fascinated me. The draughtsman asks, 'Should I paint what I see or what I know?' I thought a lot about this line when I was thinking about my painter, who I named Avílo, and I gave it to him as his central dilemma. During my research, I also discovered that Dante put narcissists in Purgatory with the counterfeiters. So, as he uses his mirror to paint (thus succumbing to the outside world, to the exterior, at the expense of the spiritual, the interior), my painter would be a vain man-of-the-world. His hopes and ideals had slipped and experience and desire had taken their place. I began to hear him talk and I wrote down what I heard. I eventually came up with eight dialogues that the painter would have with someone, each dialogue being a self-interrogation of this central dilemma. These dialogues were the first bits I wrote of *The Mirror* and the novel is built around them.

But who is he talking to? His sitter and object of his desire is Oliva, a 16-year-old novice nun, the book's narrator and illegitimate daughter of a courtesan. Another of the main things that preoccupied me from the outset was Oliva's voice. I had to get that right. As the main character, Oliva is carrying the weight of the whole book on her young shoulders and, if I didn't get her voice to sound absolutely authentic, the novel would never work. How would I get inside the head of a 16-year-old novice nun? Why on earth did I want to write from the perspective of a 16-year-old novice nun? Did I even have the right to write from the point of view of a 16-year-old novice nun? It took me a long time – several years, I would say – before I built up enough confidence in myself and gave myself permission to have a go at writing from the point of view of a young woman.

One way I found myself being able to view the world

through Oliva's eyes was via music. When I am thinking through any main character of mine, one of the things I do is build a playlist for them. For Oliva, there was one track in particular on her playlist that helped me hear her authentic voice – Plaid's remix of Björk's song "All Is Full of Love". It might seem strange and anachronistic that a mid-90s techno remix of an electronica song would match Oliva's voice, but the holy lyrics in Björk's song are the very essence of Oliva's spiritual being – it could be Oliva herself singing – and the cold, pure music fitted perfectly with the convent's world of blind windows, concealed corridors and forbidding walls that Oliva finds herself moving in.

When building a playlist for a character, the key is to seek out tracks that are deeply connected to the character's 'existential situation'. I choose those songs that best describe the inner life of the character. The songs must say something about the roots of where they come from and the core of who they are. I imagine those songs as the soundtrack to their lives. The songs will describe the character's responses to any given situation in the novel. The words of the songs are the voices inside the character's head. They are the character speaking to themselves, and us. I choose only a handful of songs – 10 at most. I listen to them on repeat shuffle and they help me to match my headspace with theirs. Only then can I write *through* character, not around them.

Another way into Oliva's voice and being, was via a few key words. In his book, *The Art of the Novel*, Milan Kundera says, 'making a character "alive" means: getting to the bottom of his existential problem. Which in turn means: getting to the bottom of some situations, some motifs, even some words that shape him.' Kundera calls these words 'theme-words'. In his novel *The Unbearable Lightness of Being*, the theme-words for the character of Tereza are: body; soul; vertigo; weakness; idyll; Paradise. For Oliva in *The Mirror*, my theme-words are: doubt; appeasement; loyalty; wonder; diminutive; old soul. These words describe fundamentally who Oliva is, the very quick of her. For me, in the writing of *The Mirror*, these theme-words acted as a focusing lens on Oliva's character.

Kundera goes on to say that, out of these six theme-words, there is usually just one that is the main key to a character. For Tereza, it was the word 'vertigo'. He said, 'I had to invent Tereza, an "experimental self", to understand vertigo.' In a similar manner, François Truffaut said that every film could be summarised in just one word – for *Last Year in Marienbad*, he said that word was 'persuasion' – and it's the same for novels. This key theme-word is almost certainly the main theme of a novel. Maybe it should even appear somehow in the novel's title. For Oliva in *The Mirror*, my key theme-word was 'doubt'. This is the root of all that Oliva does, it is her 'existential situation'.

In parallel with these explorations of Oliva's 'state of being', I also knew that I had to give her something to *do*. In an insightful essay entitled "Acting Is Doing", the film director Sydney Pollack talks about how he always tried to direct his actors to approach scenes in terms of knowing what they needed to do rather than how they should seem to be. That way, acting becomes something dynamic, active – a verb; not something adjectival, descriptive, passive. 'Acting is doing,' he said. 'Doing. Doing.' In her essay on the films of Robert Bresson, Susan Sontag talked about how 'Consciousness of the self is the "gravity" that burdens the spirit; the surpassing of the consciousness of self is "grace", or spiritual lightness.' She goes on to say that the true fight against oneself is against one's heaviness, one's gravity, and the instrument of this fight is the idea of 'work, a project, a task.' So, in *The Mirror*, Oliva would *work*. And she does. She is practically a slave labourer, and her task is to serve everybody.

When thinking about the characters around Oliva, I found the theory of the four humours to be a brilliant way in. First described by Galen in the 2nd century, the basic tenet of humourism is that the body contains four humours, or viscous liquids – blood, phlegm, black bile and yellow bile – and that the predominance of one of these humours in a person would determine their character. So, someone in whom blood was the predominant humour is described as 'sanguine' and their main characteristics would be that they are a warm person, courageous and amorous. This was an obvious description of Oliva. Someone who is 'phlegmatic' is calm and unemotional and this seemed to describe the Abbess, who maintains her cool throughout the novel, very well. A person who is 'melancholic' has a preponderance of black bile, which makes them despondent, sleepless and irritable, which is what the other novice nun in the novel, Ottavia, is like. Finally, someone who is 'choleric' is full of yellow bile and is fiery and bad-tempered.

When I was writing *The Mirror*, it wasn't obvious to me who would have this 'choleric' temperament in the book. But then something incredible happened. As I wrote, one of the nuns in the convent, Signora Pellegrina, gradually took on a greater and greater role in the story. She was very much in the background to start with, but as the story developed, so she took it upon herself to assume a much greater role, one that was extremely bad-tempered. When I started writing the book, I thought the painter, Avílo, was Oliva's enemy but, by the time I had finished writing the book, I realised that it was, in fact, Pellegrina. She had stepped forward and was Oliva's true nemesis. She is a monster. It was one of those wonderful moments in writing when a character completely takes over and asserts themselves whether the writer likes it or not.

In thinking about these characters surrounding Oliva, I realised that they were not only characters in themselves but they were also aspects of Oliva's personality. For Oliva, the Abbess represents everything that is good in the convent. Oliva adores and worships the Abbess whole-heartedly. Oliva, on the other hand, greatly fears Pellegrina, whose mission in the convent is to persecute and punish Oliva. Ottavia's challenging of her cloistered life and her eventual departure from it pulls on Oliva's own sense of doubt. Finally, the painter arrives in the convent as the devil come to plant the seed of temptation in Oliva's mind (the painter's name, Avílo, is a deliberate mirroring of Oliva's). As Oliva moves through the numerous rooms within the convent, she encounters these characters, these aspects of her personality, and the rooms exist as zones of her feelings. These characters, and their presences in the convent, turn the convent into a kind of Rorschach drawing of Oliva's personality.

As well as setting and voice, the third main thing that preoccupied me from the outset was plot. Because the setting was so static, I knew I had to ramp up the plot. We were going nowhere in terms of space, so the time element in the story had to move like a rocket. During the time I was thinking through the story of *The Mirror*, I always asked myself, 'What if…? What if…?' I made notes on bits of paper of all of these possible story-events. After five years, I had a box full of them. I poured them onto the floor and sorted through them. There were lots of repetitions, lots of notes that were clearly irrelevant, but a slow sorting through gradually revealed a storyline. I moved the bits of paper around. What if that event went there, not there? How would that change things? Finding the right places for these bits of paper plugged huge holes in the plot.

The fundamental theme-word for Oliva was 'doubt', so I knew that there would be a great deal of conflict within Oliva herself, but I also made sure that there was conflict between her and some of the other nuns, most obviously Pellegrina. Then there was conflict between the nuns themselves, who were split into those who wanted a stricter conventual life and those who didn't. Finally, there was huge conflict between the convent and the state, represented in the novel by the Magistrate and the Bishop. These patriarchs wanted to re-assert their control over the nuns but, led by the Abbess, they try to assert their independence. So, there was conflict on as many levels as I could think of – within and between people and the city's institutions.

When I was plotting *The Mirror*, there was one book in particular that I learned a great deal from – Henry James' *The Turn of the Screw*. James' book is a masterclass on how to ratchet up the tension in a story. As we move through the story, so the plot tightens and tightens and sends the reader spiralling ever-upwards. By the end of the book, the plot has twisted the story so tightly that we are left hanging in a crescendo in mid-air. Everything in *The Turn of the Screw* happens on the last page and the ending is left highly ambiguous. James wrote the book as an attempt to write a potboiler after a friend challenged him. The title itself refers to this ratcheting up of the tension in the story. It's an incredible book and I tried to follow James' model for my story. Each death in *The Mirror* is a point of no return for Oliva and marks a moment of her increasing panic. By the end of the story, Oliva has no allies left and no way out. When I started writing *The Mirror*, I didn't know how it would end. It was only as I was approaching the end that the actual ending came to me. I simply had no idea that such a sudden and violent act was how the book would end. It was deeply shocking to me but, of course, looking back over how I plotted it, the story couldn't have ended any other way. The highly ambiguous ending was both surprising and yet inevitable.

While thinking through the story of *The Mirror*, there were two other books that I drew on for inspiration. The first of these was Charlotte Perkins Gilman's *The Yellow Wallpaper*, with its cries and whispers from beyond the walls. From it, I learned a great deal about how to write from the point of view of a woman on the verge of a nervous breakdown. JL Carr's *A Month in the Country*, in which the narrator uncovers and identifies with the figure in the mural with her 'flaming red hair', was equally useful. But, as with all my other novels, the true inspiration behind *The Mirror* wasn't another book, but a film – Powell and Pressburger's *Black Narcissus*.

Released in 1947, the film concerns a group of nuns who try to establish a convent high up in the Himalayas. However, as soon as they arrive, their aim is constantly thwarted, first by the wind, lethargy and ill-health, then by the local people, then by the return of memories long banished and mental disintegration, and finally by the eruption of sexual desire. Although shot entirely in a studio, the film's setting is breathtaking, created using a series of painted glass backdrops, and this setting acts as the main character, absorbing and dissolving all presences into itself so that, ultimately, all that is left is an erotic landscape of the mind.

The film works as a play of oppositions: melodrama vs art-house West vs East; Ariel vs Caliban; parent vs child; Sister Clodagh vs Sister Ruth; chastity vs sexuality; white vs red. This last motif is, visually speaking, the movie's central and most striking image. The nuns wear off-white habits and no make-up, which makes their faces seem white and bloodless and so, in the scene when Sister Ruth confronts Sister Clodagh with her red dress and bright red lipstick and then goes on her lost, labyrinthine creep around the convent, the effect is all the more shocking.

Like Powell's film, I made sure to 'colour-code' *The Mirror* very carefully. In Venice, there is very little greenery and so the colour green plays very little part in the novel. The main colours in *The Mirror* are blue and yellow – the colour of the sky and sun (which is all that Oliva can see beyond the walls of the convent). They also happen to be the Madonna's colours.

The only other colour to make an appearance is red, but it appears only in connection with Oliva's sexuality – when she sees red pantaloons in a painting, when the painter spreads crushed cinnamon on her lips or when she has her period. When Octavia escapes the convent, Oliva refers to her as a 'red bird' flying away. Set against the bare walls of the convent, the colour leaps out at the reader and acts as an alarm bell, a siren, alerting us that Oliva is in danger of becoming sexually aroused.

I spent five years planning *The Mirror*. In that time, I was turning the story over and over in my mind, thinking through the story again and again, letting it build and build inside me. I think novels grow rather like planets – ideas slowly amass and gradually coalesce to form something more and more solid so that, ultimately, it's hard to know when a novel 'starts' and your self ends. When it came to the actual writing, *The Mirror* only took three months to write and not one word was changed in the editing process. The only reason the novel came out so cleanly was because of the five years I spent planning it. It was one of the most weird and wonderful writing experiences I will ever have. I love Oliva.

DAVID BOWIE OUTLAW BY ALEX SHARPE

DYLAN Jones' oral biography, *David Bowie: A Life*, with its multiple voices, like tesserae, paints a wonderfully warm portrait of the man, but if you're looking for a book that analyses Bowie's work in new, fresh ways, then Alex Sharpe's book, *David Bowie Outlaw* is the one. Quite simply, it is the most insightful book I've read that pulls out the preoccupations, the poses and the patterns that flow through David Bowie's life and work. Most books on Bowie's career tend to look at the individual albums, or events, as sources of ideas, but Sharpe employs a much more original approach, looking at the life and work through a series of five lenses: difference, authenticity, ethics, art and love. As a Professor of Law, Sharpe's approach is to cast her expert eye over the ways in which Bowie flirted with, challenged or transgressed the sociological, cultural and ethical norms of the day. In each of the (beautifully succinct) essays, she quotes liberally from interviews with Bowie, other writers on Bowie, as well song lyrics and artwork, showing us that these preoccupations, poses and patterns weren't located in different, discrete places but were, in fact, spread across the *whole* of his life and work, thus in each essay drawing together Bowie's life and work into a single entity.

In the first essay, 'Difference', Sharpe considers how Bowie has always been 'otherworldly'. Just think of all the formal acting roles he played: alien (Nicholas Roeg's *The Man Who Fell to Earth*), degenerate (Bertolt Brecht's *Baal* on the BBC), vampire (*The Hunger*), freak (*The Elephant Man* on Broadway) as well as the off-screen characters he inhabited and performed: Ziggy, Aladdin Sane, Halloween Jack, the Thin White Duke, Pierrot. She goes on to make the case that Bowie was, in fact, a kind of monster (from the Latin, *monstrare,* meaning to show, demonstrate*),* a figure in cultural history that can be read as an 'amalgam of fear and desire', a sign of things to come, a future full of surprise.

In the essay entitled 'Art', Sharpe looks at how Bowie stole the idea of the cut-up from William Burroughs, whom he famously met in 1974, and how he employed the process in his own work, particularly on *Diamond Dogs.* She says that Burroughs and Bowie 'were visionaries: provocateurs, collaborators, dedicated thieves' and that the cut-ups 'operate as a circuit breaker, a jammer', bringing us closer to how life actually presents itself to us as 'a series of interruptions and random juxtapositions'.

In the final essay, simply called 'Love', Sharpe examines Bowie's lifelong interest in specific religions (Tibetan Buddhism, Christianity, Judaism) and in spirituality more generally (Gnosticism, Kabbalism). She argues that the song, 'Loving the Alien', is in fact about spiritual questing, the alien being a metaphor for God. Bowie himself agreed: '[T]his song is not, it may surprise you to know, another ode to little green Martians.' Sharpe suggests that the clearest expression of this side to Bowie is found on *Heathen,* an album which Bowie said was about 'somebody who has lowered his standards, spiritually, intellectually, morally ... someone who's not even bothered searching for a spiritual life anymore, who completely exists on a materialistic plain.'

But it is in the second essay, entitled 'Authenticity', that Sharpe presents for me the most thrilling, clever and convincing case regarding Bowie's status as an artist. Emerging in the era of confessional singer-songwriters like Dylan, Neil Young & Joni Mitchell, Bowie's work was often accused of being inauthentic. Those singers sang in an authentic voice, some said, whereas Bowie's work was all masks and role playing, but Bowie understood the difference between authenticity and truth. Sharpe states, 'Bowie's work is truthful as opposed to authentic', and goes on to say, 'he refused to penetrate audiences with his truth. Rather, through self-consciously donning masks, he sought to create spaces in which audience members could create and express their own truths.' Sharpe makes the point that there is no authoritative voice in Bowie's work, only multiple readings. In privileging surface over depth, truth over authenticity, Bowie was essentially an actor. Bowie himself said, 'I have no message whatsoever. I really have nothing to say, no suggestions or advice, nothing.'

The argument she makes in this section is one of the most elegant insights into Bowie-as-artist that I have ever come across and is just one of many, many more that you will encounter in this beautifully-structured and extremely well-written book. Chapeau!

A MAP TOWARDS FLUENCY BY LISA KELLY

WALTER Benjamin said that 'Work on a good piece of writing proceeds on three levels: a musical one, where it is composed; an architectural one, where it is constructed; and a textile one, where it is woven' and it's that final word, 'woven', that I can't stop thinking about as I read Lisa Kelly's work. Her debut collection is a fine fabric shop displaying the most wonderful array of fabric weight, pattern, design hue, intensity, transparency, degrees of brilliance and surface contour.

The book is divided into seven sections, with titles such as 'Scale and Accuracy', 'Coordinates', 'Navigation', all of which build up and add to the sense that the book is a map of Kelly's own life and life experiences thus far. A poem in the first of these sections, entitled "ø", perhaps best sums up Kelly's intentions for her project, dealing as it does with the fact that she is 'half-Danish and half-deaf':

> Danish for island
> a new word
> new world
> to explore
>
> My tongue
> tastes the sound of ø
> touches its shores
> its limits

A later section, titled 'Orientation', deals explicitly with Kelly's difficulty in hearing and speaking – the words 'tongue' and 'ear' pop up all over the place and the poem after which the collection is named cleverly traces Kelly's own struggle to learn British Sign Language.

But it is the sheer verve and poise of all of Kelly's poems that really impresses. Above all, Kelly is an inventive, playful poet, most of all with form. The first poem of hers that I ever came across was "And I Have Seen", which deals with the consequences of fracking and the gases that it releases, which can catch fire on rivers and kill fish species. The poem is written as a preacher's warning of the oncoming apocalypse and plays with biblical images and primal colours – orange, black. Words are repeated, building a strong sense of prophecy and doom, and lines are put in a specular form, but the form isn't exact, which keeps it feeling organic rather than a dry exercise.

Another formal tour de force is "This Is Not a Road Trip". The setting is a large bay in south Brittany, in which various things are happening at once – a boy is throwing a stone into the sea, a horse rider crosses the sand, a fisherman comes in with full nets. Overlooking the bay is a house, in which the Minaut family live. The son, Patrick, has just died and the poem begins with this statement. Kelly holds each event separately and then connects them all in the bay, rather like the separate elements in a Miró painting that inter-relate, or like Auden's "Musée des Beaux Arts", in which tragedy goes unnoticed and life carries on. The form of the poem, with elements repeating, and lines gradually indented and then pulled back to the margin, create a wave-like motion which reflects its setting. This poem is remarkable for its symmetry, its inward tension and its balance.

There are several poems that are made up of parts, or sequences of poems, in the collection, including the extraordinary "Apple Quartet" – is there anything more gorgeous in the English language than a list of the names of the different kinds of apple? Another sequence of poems is "Coronas/Cuts", actually a crown of sonnets that deftly weaves lines and images from John Donne's work into Kelly's own moving meditation on the inevitability of sons leaving home and, startlingly, on knife crime.

Kelly also uses herself and her family as subjects for her poems. "Six Perspectives on Lilian Kjærulff", for example, is a series of six views on the poet's mother from different familial perspectives – 'second daughter from a second marriage', 'first husband', etc. The result is a clever and intriguing Cubist portrait of a woman who nevertheless retains an air of mystery and elusivness. "Clavical: snaps", ostensibly about a cycling accident Kelly was involved in, morphs into a wider discussion on mortality by referencing David Cronenberg's *Crash*, the Japanese tradition of Kintsugi (the repairing of broken pots using gold) and the myth of Apollo and Daphne.

Other poems that deserve a special mention are the moving "Let Them Leave Language to Their Lonely Betters", the deeply mysterious "Saltatorium" and the melancholy of "Aubade for an Artist", but I could go on and on. For me, a great many debut collections tend to have a lot of filler in them, but not so with Kelly. The core strength of the work is impressively maintained from beginning to end. There are more ideas per page here than most collections of poetry could only dream of and it will be an absolute travesty if *A Map Towards Fluency* doesn't win a major prize in the coming year.

IN AN IDEAL WORLD I'D NOT BE MURDERED
BY CHAUCER CAMERON

THE epigraph says it all: To my dearest Helen & [   ]. This magnificent book, part memoir and part fiction of the author's experiences in the sex industry, exists to give voice to those muted and a presence to those prostitutes murdered. As a novelist as well as a poet, I'm obsessed with the issues of voice and point of view and Chaucer Cameron's book uses these two devices expertly and very effectively. The book is so rich with the choices she has made with regard to POV and the way she deploys voice. The book sings with them.

In many of the poems – "Body Marks" and parts I-III of "King's Cross Café" for example – Cameron's narrator acts as a kind of camera/recorder, capturing snippets of hard-won advice, complaints of injuries inflicted by punters, the banter between women at work. In "Trixie Is a Whore", the first-person narrator is a 'customer,, evaluating his own prowess with Trixie because of how quickly he can make her urinate with his finger and gauging her (very young) age according to how "tight" she is.

A poem like "Erotic" (set out as a series of long columns, like the poles the narrator dances on) reads like a short story. The narrator reminisces that "Back in '82 / there were / no poles to / slither down" before going on to describe her mundane thoughts during one of her performances. The poem continues with the owner taking her out for dinner, but this is no act of charity - the owner wants something in return and gets it as he watches "the light / in my / acid eyes / go out / just before / they / close." That last line.

In what I think may be the most powerful poem in the collection, "Coup de Maître", the act of devouring a shellfish is made explicitly like the act of emotional evisceration during paid sex. The power is only one way and it is a brutal, total destruction. I found it a very difficult poem to read, but a necessary one, of course.

The large cast of characters in the book include Crystal with her switchblades, Ellen who is murdered on the Green, Caprice, Eve, Morgan, Grace, Ash (so important that these women are given their names and their stories recorded). These poems are set in a hellish hall of mirrors, but instead of reflections, what the reader is presented with are vulnerabilities, desperation, fear. These women have no choices available to them at all but, even within their devastating world, there are small victories and moments of relief, comedy even: "'That is Jaen,' says Crystal, pointing towards the sleeping woman. 'J A E N, not Jayne with a Y, or even plain Jane, but, J A E N, for god's sake, talk about making life hard'."

As a white, middle-class male, I cannot even begin to imagine what it must have been like for Cameron to survive in this world. But survive she did and I think her greatest achievement is being as brave as she so clearly has been to return to it once more to give voice where there was none and give these women some dignity and respect. There will be plenty of books of poetry that grab the headlines and win prizes this year, but none of them will be as important as this one.

A FIRE SHARED BY PETER DIDSBURY

I came to know about this book through the ever-excellent series of close readings of poems that Carol Rumens posts for the Guardian. The poem by Didsbury she looked at was the eponymous "A Fire Shared", about which she said: 'Didsbury is a writer whose historical imagination and linguistic awareness illuminate a poetry of unusual reach and resonance.' Well, that got me interested and so I bought a copy. Rumens went on to say that Didsbury is 'often a poet of borders – between lyric and narrative, comedy and tragedy, fantastic and and realistic.' Reading through the 38 poems in the collection, I couldn't agree more.

The first thing I noticed about the poems was how many of them concern themselves with daily domestic life. The viewpoint of many of the poems – "The Fog", "Stepping Outside", "Language And Land" – is inside a house looking out into the garden, which then takes on mystical or fantastical overtones. In "A Pasture For Gazelles", for instance, the narrator says,

> The dog lies on the lawn, cracking open a peach stone I'm sure I
> remember tossing onto that flower bed years ago, long before he
> was born.

In "Eleven a.m", the "end of the garden" stands in a "blue religious haze". In "The Evening Star", the narrator says: "Walking these gardens I have lately come to perceive / The firmament as something that observes me, / A scrutinising Face…" These domestic-pastoral poems are just lovely, raising as they do the everyday to the ecstatic.

The Surrealists placed a near-sacredness on everyday objects and, at times, Didsbury's work verges on the surreal. Not the

Surrealism of Breton or Ernst, but the softer surrealism of Leonora Carrington or Leonor Fini. More whimsy, flights of fancy and zaniness than hardcore Surrealist. "Yellow Shoes", for example, is a curtal sonnet about a journey into an Oz-like land, but many of the poems are infused with such Lewis Carroll-like logic. There is one poem in particular, the hilarious "Tweedles", that explicitly references Lewis Carroll:

> while Dum and Dee
> in their lunatic pomp and gear
> come jousting either side of the fence
> before falling off their giddy-up broomstick chargers
> and rolling around in the grass.

Then there is Didsbury's obvious love of balladry and social history. It comes as no surprise to learn that he is a highly experienced archaeologist. The wonderfully titled "Braxy-Hams", for instance, tells the ballad of a "moorland lover" who wishes to win his love by giving her some braxy hams (defined in the Scottish Gallovidian Encyclopaedia as 'the hams of those sheep which die of the braxy'). It is very whimsical. The equally weird and wonderful "Bevis of Hampton" tells the story of a figure long lost in the mists of time who "sate upon a hill. / Beneath a tree, on a February day. / And all his food was a green goose, oh." That "green goose" is just genius and the whole thing is very funny.

Indeed, there is the sense in Didsbury's world that the past, or the paranormal, is never far away. The poems are never surprised when ghosts and visitations make their appearance. The quality of living so long in other dreamy worlds brings with it an occasional amnesiac-like confusion of time and place. In "Lines of Enquiry", the narrator is asked by a stranger what day of the week it is. His reply is, "I'm really surprised by his Dorset accent, / so it takes me a while, but Friday, / definitely Friday." The book closes with just such a poem, "Homeward Bound", in which the narrator says:

> On this seemingly endless avenue
> it depends upon how you align yourself
> with regard to the trees
> as to how much exhaustion you feel

But, for me, what is most impressive in Didsbury's work is his microscopic attention to detail in the natural world. Nowhere is this more evident than in the truly cosmic poem "Words At Wharram Percy", which was originally published in the TLS and was once projected onto the Royal Festival Hall. In the poem, the narrator observes:

> Low-skimming birds pick flies from the tensile
> surface of the pond, and each touch rings
> as if struck from a vanished bell.
> Hillside pasture lies fizzing under the rain,
> through which a partridge
> hurries her brood to safety
> among cowslip, oat grass, Yorkshire fog, black medick.

This poem wouldn't look out of place in Geoffrey Hill's *Mercian Hymns* with its telescopic look back through time to a wife who calls out "in Middle English, / to a man who mows in the glebe". All of the natural world and its history falls into this magnificent poem. It is, perhaps, the finest poem in the book, a book which is elsewhere also packed with bright and beautiful things.

SELECTED POEMS BY DONALD DAVIE

DONALD Davie is an odd one for me. I want to like the body of his work much more than I do, but there are a dozen or so poems by him that I like as much as, if not more than, anyone else's. Those poems were among the first poems I took very much to heart when I started to read and write poetry more seriously in my late teens, early twenties. For me, there is no finer poem than Davie's 'Ezra Pound in Pisa'. I found these poems in his *Selected Poems*, published by Carcanet in 1985 – a book with a dull red cover that I came across in a second-hand bookshop. The choices were Davie's own, which made it an even more interesting selection. Imagine my surprise and dismay, then, when I turned to the contents page of Sinéad Morrissey's choices for this new *Selected Poems* to find 'Ezra Pound in Pisa' and many other of those amazing poems missing. To be fair to Morrissey, she does say that her selection is 'highly personal' and should only be used as a starting point into Donald Davie's huge oeuvre, with which I wholeheartedly agree.

Born to Baptist parents in Barnsley in 1922, Donald Davie won a scholarship to Barnsley Holgate Grammar School and then, in 1940, won a place at St Catharine's College, Cambridge to read English. A spell in the Royal Navy during the war interrupted his degree but he returned to Cambridge and completed his BA, MA and PhD there. He spent 20-odd years teaching at a series of prestigious universities in England, Ireland and the United States. Despite his many years spent abroad in a variety of countries, however, Davie remained an Englishman at heart. His publisher, Michael Schmidt, once differentiated between two kinds of expat.

There were those, like Davie's friend Thom Gunn, who shed their skins and assimilated themselves thoroughly and wholeheartedly into their new culture. The other kind, however, do not; instead the old country looms larger than ever and is longed for even more keenly. Davie was the latter kind. He wrote 'The Shires', a poem for every county in England, while living in California, for example.

Concerning his life as a poet, Davie himself said that he was 'not a poet by nature, only by inclination; for my mind moves most easily and happily among abstractions, it relates ideas far more readily than it relates experiences.' His poetry can err on the side of didacticism so that we often get a report of an event plus its significance, rather than just the event itself. He is the antithesis of William Carlos William's dictum 'no ideas but in things'. This is illustrated very clearly and well in the opening line of his 1955 poem, 'Poem as Abstract': 'A poem is less an orange than a grid;'. This abstract side to his writing found fuller expression in his role as a critic. As a critic, Davie was extremely prolific, writing two books on Ezra Pound and many essays on Hardy and Lawrence, Robert Graves, David Jones and other First World War poets, Basil Bunting, and then later figures such as Hugh MacDiarmid, Roy Fisher, Charles Tomlinson, Geoffrey Hill and Ted Hughes. While his reviews might not be up there in such august company as T.S. Eliot or William Empson, or Coleridge before them, they do show a pretty comprehensive knowledge and understanding of contemporary American, European and Slavic poetry.

Davie's early poetry showed a steadfast adherence to traditional, conventional forms, relying heavily on regular metre and end-rhyme. But, as he got older, he took on board the influences of his readings into the Modernism of Pound and Bunting (about whom he also wrote a book) plus, occasionally, the freer, looser style of American poets like Frank O'Hara and the American

Objectivists, whose work he encountered during his many years in the US. Surprisingly, when it was published by Carcanet in 1989, he even wrote an overall favourable review of *A Various Art*, an anthology of British postmodern poets including J. H. Prynne and Douglas Oliver, edited by Andrew Crozier and Tim Longville. Most of all, however, Davie sought inspiration and instruction from a whole host of Slavic and Russian poets, Czeslaw Miloz and Boris Pasternak in particular (Davie was stationed in Russia during the war, taught himself the language and read Russian poetry in the original).

But, however enthusiastic he was about *Briggflatts* or the *Cantos*, Davie could never reach those dizzy heights of compression, expression and erudition. His poetry always retained a cosy, conservative feel. The modernist strain in Davie's later work is the strain that speaks most to me. In these freer poems, Davie frequently rejects end-rhyme, regular line length, etc, and instead pilots and lands the poems in unusual and unexpected places. His amazing poem 'The 'Sculpture' of Rhyme', for example, ends with the line: 'And a mouth to graze on feldspar.'; while 'Gardens no Emblems' ends thusly:

> But forms of thought move in another plane
> Whose matrices no natural forms afford
> Unless subjected to prodigious strain:
> Say, light proceeding edgewise, like a sword.

Indeed, it is this conflict between the concrete and abstract (the orange vs the grid) that runs throughout Davie's work and, therefore, I would say is its defining feature.

After many years in the US, Davie returned to Britain in 1988 and, the following year, he published his final volume of poems, *To Scorch or Freeze*. Written after Davie had converted to Anglicanism, *To Scorch or Freeze* takes its cue from the Psalms and, technically speaking, from Pound's *Cantos*. It is a late flowering of religious meditations riddled, as it should be, with doubt and contradictions. As Davie's own *Selected Poems* had come out in 1985, one advantage Morrissey's selection has over Davie's is that she is able to include poems from that collection. Indeed, she chooses more poems from *To Scorch or Freeze* than any other of Davie's collections. Shortly before his death in 1995, Davie wrote one last poem, a sequence entitled 'Our Father', often thought of as the finest of his religious poems. Another advantage of Morrissey's selection over Davie's is that she is able to include this, too, in her selection.

Davie's output is truly astounding in its range and volume – his *Collected Poems* alone runs to more than 600 pages – but, to my mind anyway, I feel he never really got a grasp on where he stood stylistically. Torn between the conservatism of Hardy on one side and the radicalness of Pound on the other; drawing on the dry, dusty Augustans as well as the free jazz of late 20th-century American poetry, Davie never really found the right footing. His masterpiece is almost certainly *Essex Poems 1963-67*, composed during a happy time in his life when he was Chair of Essex University. He covered so much ground over such a long period of time that there will undoubtedly be something for everyone in his work. Sinéad Morrissey's *Selected Poems* provides a good tour round the decades of Davie's life as a poet but, for me, it is those dozen or so poems first encountered when I was a teenager that continue to ring through the ages.

ALAIN TANNER – AN APPRECIATION

I'VE just found out that, two days before Jean-Luc Godard died on 13 September 2022, the Swiss filmmaker Alain Tanner also passed away. This is especially ironic because, with Godard, Tanner's early films shared a radical political agenda. As part of my undergraduate English Literature & Film degree, we were forced to study how form conveyed political meaning in the films *Pierrot le fou*, *Weekend* and *Tout va bien*. It was pretty tortuous. However, whereas Godard's films quickly descended into an ill-thought-through Marxism, Tanner's agenda in his early films was far more fully expressed and could therefore connect to a much wider audience. Maybe this was partly due to the fact that a couple of those early movies of his were written in collaboration with John Berger.

After he made *Messidor* in 1977 (a controversial road movie about two young woman who kill a man after he tries to sexually assault them), Tanner had a heart attack followed by heart surgery. Afterwards, he said he was through making didactic movies and emerged a few years later with *Light Years Away*, his first movie in English. This was in 1981 and the film marked my entry point into Tanner's work. As an impressionable 16-year old, I remember watching it late one night on Channel Four. I vaguely remember it being set in a dilapidated petrol station in a post-apocalyptic world. The cast – including Trevor Howard and Mick Ford – was dressed in rags and there was a big bird which seemed to hold some great significance. It bemused me but I never forgot it.

So, when his next movie came out a few years later, I went to see it in the cinema. The film was *In the White City* and it made a deep impression on me that lasts to this day. The story is simplicity itself: a mechanic on an oil tanker, capriciously decides to jump ship at Lisbon. He spends the following few months wandering around the 'white' city, filming himself and everything he sees – the streets, tram rides, the sea – on a Super-8 camera. He sends these home movies to a woman (his wife?) in Switzerland, who has them developed and watches them. They are postcards from a man who is frozen in time and place, a *flâneur* who has no aim and no agenda, a sailor anchored on the road to nowhere.

Nothing much happens in the movie. It is dreamy, largely without event or incident and therefore plotless. It was no surprise to learn that the film was completely improvised by Tanner and his lead actor Bruno Ganz. The film carries no screenplay credit. The pleasure of the film comes from this aimlessness. It's a film about the moment, the here and now, without care or comment. Is the sailor having an existential crisis or has he found himself at last? We never know, but that's not the point. On the aforementioned undergraduate degree, I wrote a paper on Tanner's film and its use of those home movies. The movies are an exploration of space, not time, and so they 'freeze' us and force us jump out of the story, just as the sailor has jumped ship and is landlocked. The home movies gradually replace the film's story-time itself as the nameless sailor's being dissolves into the surfaces of the city – the stone, the breeze, the water, the white light and dust.

In the same year that *In the White City* was released, Andrei Tarkovsky released his movie *Nostalgia*, a film with which Tanner's bears a lot of similarities. In Tarkovsky's movie, the main character (played by the late great Oleg Jankovsky) is also existentially 'stuck'. Tarkovsky's movie is devoid of plot, too. Set in and around the Roman baths of a small Tuscan town, the main events are a nosebleed, a rainfall, an argument, lighting a candle. Nothing happens and then it's all over. Wonderful.

A couple of years later, Agnès Varda released her stunning movie *Vagabond*, in which Sandrine Bonnaire plays a young itinerant woman called Mona who, when asked why she drifts around so much, simply shrugs her shoulders and replies, 'I move.' The film is a series of gazes, of one-way exchanges from different people – dropouts, hippies, a prostitute, an itinerant worker, a maid – but each of these 'witnesses' is not seeing Mona, but a reflection of their own regrets, secrets, longings. Mona is the blank centre of the film and she leaves no trace of her existence.

All three of these movies are about characters in a state of self-imposed exile and all contain highly-choreographed tracking shots. For me, they form a loose trilogy of road movies, but of a distinctively European kind rather than, say, *Easy Rider*. When I saw these movies in the cinema, I was too young to fully appreciate their subtlety and sophistication. They are 'writerly' films – films that explore contingent states of being – rather than 'readerly' films, which rely on the idea of causality in plot. When I started to write fiction, I remembered Tanner's film in particular. It taught me that you can write in real time, about inconsequential things, such as corners of rooms, billowing curtains, a night in a bar, the heat of the sun, a wall. Just moments, things, nothing more. We don't have to be a slave to plot. It was a revelation.

I was fortunate to meet and interview Tanner once, in the early '90s, when his movie *The Diary of Lady M* was screened at the BFI in London. He told me a story that evening which I've never forgotten. Some time in the '70s, in between film projects, he mounted a camera facing outwards on his car window and drove around his native Switzerland for days and days letting the camera run and run. He edited the footage down to around 8 hours of film of roadside views of streets, trees, houses, lakes, supermarkets, mountains, petrol stations, etc. He organised an evening with friends to show them the footage. After all 8 hours, every one of his friends was numb with boredom and they all urged him never to release any of it. He said he'd never been so disappointed with a reaction in his life. I laughed when he told me that story because I would have loved that film. A great artist, massively overlooked and severely underrated. *Merci*, Alain. *Adieu*.

EISENSTEIN'S 'MONTAGE OF ATTRACTIONS'

EVERY Wednesday morning at 9am sharp, I would be in the main lecture hall at Sussex University about to start watching a film. I was doing an English Literature degree there, and was advised to attend as my course had a minor in film, but anyone could attend. Of course, hardly anyone did. Trying to get humanities students into a lecture hall at 9am is a snowball's chance in Hell. So, myself and a scattering of others watched movies like *Yeelen* (the Bambara word for 'brightness') directed by Souleymane Cissé, *Weekend* by Jean-Luc Godard (baffling) and *The Colour of Pomegranates* by Sergei Parajanov (incredible). At the end of Parajanov's movie, I remember one person stood up and applauded, and for good reason – once seen, never forgotten. Another movie I saw at that ungodly hour was *Strike* by Sergei Mikhailovich Eisenstein.

I knew of Eisenstein of course – such a famous name – but I was shamefully ignorant of his films. *Strike* hit me like a hammer blow with its final images of the massacre of striking workers by the Czarist police cut together with documentary shots of a bull's death in an abattoir. Wow. Powerful stuff. Luckily for me, Sussex kept many other of Eisenstein's movies on video tape, which you could book to watch on a monitor in a small booth. So off I went and watched *Battleship Potemkin* and *October*, both of which were made up of equally striking images and startling cuts. I was hooked. I explored.

When the Bolshevik Revolution started in 1917, Eisenstein was a student at the Institute of Civil Engineering in Petrograd. He was 19 years old. The Revolution smashed the co-ordinates of his life, bringing about the dissolution of his family as his parents departed into exile, but it also gave him the opportunity to produce himself anew. He was conscripted in 1919 and sent to the Red Army's School for Ensigns. He abandoned his plan to become an engineer – his father's profession – and saw that the nascent art form of cinema could be a vehicle for political propaganda and a laboratory for avant-grade experiment. In order to achieve this, he strove to become an intellectual, to construct for himself a new world-view, a new ideological conception of both society and of art. He had to become a student of aesthetics in order to work in the cinema.

In 1920, after a period in the Red Army, Lev Kuleshov became a teacher at the State Film School, where he set up his own workshop. It was there that Kuleshov carried out his famous experiments in editing. The most famous of these involved cutting together a close-up of the face of an actor called Ivan Ilyich Mozhukhin with other shots, variously reported as shots of soup, a dead woman, a baby. The result was that the audience immediately assumed that the actor's expression had changed although the close-up used each time was the same. So the expression perceived on an actor's face – hunger, grief, joy, etc. – is determined by the shots which precede and follow it.

Eisenstein studied under Kuleshov for three months in 1923. He took Kuleshov's idea and developed it further. As a Marxist, Eisenstein believed that the law of the dialectical conflict and synthesis of opposites could provide principles of dynamic editing. Thus he deliberately opposed himself to continuity editing; he sought out and exploited what Hollywood would call 'discontinuities'. He staged, shot, and cut his early films for the maximum collision from shot to shot, sequence to sequence, since he believed that only through being forced to synthesize such conflicts does the viewer participate in a dialectical process. Eisenstein sought to make the collisions and conflicts not only perceptual but also emotional and intellectual. His aim was nothing less than to alter the audience's total consciousness.

Eisenstein came up with a phrase to describe this guiding aesthetic principle in his early films, he called it the 'montage of attractions'. In his book, *The Film Sense*, he writes:

> 'Don't forget it was a young engineer who was bent on finding a scientific approach to the secrets and mysteries of art. The disciplines he had studied had taught him one thing: in every scientific investigation there must be a unit of measurement. So he set out in search of the unit of impression produced by art! Science knows 'ions', 'electrons' and 'neutrons'. Let there be 'attraction' in art. Everyday language borrowed from industry a word denoting the assembling of machinery, pipes, machine tools. This striking word is 'montage' which means assembling. Very well! Let units of impression combined into one whole be expressed through a dual term, half-industrial and half-music-hall. Thus was the term 'montage of attractions' coined.'

The meaning generated in the field of consciousness of the spectator while they watched Kuleshov's experiments in editing were generated *across the cut*, not in any single, neutral image. Ah-ha, I thought, here is a tool that sparks an idea in the viewer's mind, an idea that is not present in any single image. It's the combination of two images that creates something else, something new, something that hadn't existed before. So, it's not so much about the selection of images that creates meaning, but the *combination* of them. Montage suggests an idea by means of metaphor, an association of ideas. It is an aesthetic 'transformer'. What precedes the cut should attract what follows it, and vice versa. The energy of this attraction could derive from a contrast, a comparison or a repetition. In this way, the cut acts like the 'hinge of a metaphor' (my phrase).

At the same time as Eisenstein was pursuing his theory of montage in cinema, the Russian Formalists were also striving to bring a scientific critical rigour in their approach to their field of study – literature. Indeed, many artists, or 'cultural workers', of the period took their cue from the work on literary theory of the Formalists. In particular, Viktor Shklovsky's idea of 'making strange' (*ostranenie*) is a concept that shares much with the ideas behind montage cinema. Between 1923 and 1928, there existed a loose association of artists and critics from the Futurist, Constructivist and Formalist movements called the Russian Left Front of the Arts. This group published an avant-grade journal, *Lef*, for which Eisenstein contributed some essays.

At the same time that I was learning about Eisenstein, I was reading about the Formalists, especially the work of Roman Jakobson, who was two years older than Eisenstein. Jakobson's great contribution to Formalism was his idea of the 'metaphoric and metonymic axes' of language. Jakobson sees metaphor and metonymy as the modes that underpin the two-fold process of *selection* and *combination* of language. Sentences are constructed by the 'vertical' movement of selecting particular words from our inner storehouse of language and then by combining them into the 'horizontal' movement of a sentence. This vertical axis is metaphoric; the horizontal metonymic. Metaphor operates via association whereas metonymy is syntagmatic. Jakobson concluded, "In poetry, the line of least resistance is metaphor; for prose, metonymy."

If we apply Jakobson's theories to Eisenstein's use of montage, we can see that his early films are clearly more poetic than prosaic because they operate more via metaphor, not metonymy. A simple montage of 'a shot of a deer + a shot of a twig snapping = fear' is an obvious prosaic connotation, but the scene in *Strike* when a factory boss uses a lemon squeezer as the police move in on striking workers is a combination of two images that bear no intrinsic connection to each other. Rather than describing it as a connotation, I'd say the type of montage Eisenstein pioneered is a 'harsh juxtaposition'. Editing in Eisenstein's early movies is usually more important than any desire to construct a coherent fictional space and time. Narrative flow tends to be subordinated to film image.

At the same time that I was learning about montage and Formalism, I was just starting to write fiction. The idea of the 'montage of attractions' was a revelation to me and it is a principle that I have carried with me throughout my life as a writer. The idea of 'making connections' is one of the best definitions I know of what writing is really all about. This is what EM Forster meant when he said, 'Only connect.' Always be making the connection, even, and especially, when two images or sentences seem to have no connection at all.

In 2015, a collection of my essays, *Vade Mecum*, was published by Zer0 Books. In it was an essay entitled "Flickers" in which I took the idea of the montage of attractions to its fullest possible conclusion. I sampled the whole history of cinema into an essay made up entirely of bits and pieces. It ends thusly:

Hal Hartley's comment that there is no such thing as adventure and romance, there's only trouble and desire. Jean-Luc Godard: 'All you need to make a movie is a girl and a gun'. Bergman's *Cries and Whispers* as adult *verité*. The whole of Ingmar Bergman's output. Scorsese is to Michael Powell as Spielberg is to David Lean. Cameras, watches, headlamps, spectacles and binoculars in *Chinatown*. The flaw in Faye Dunaway's eye in *Chinatown*. The essential question in *The Draughtsman's Contract* – should an artist draw what he sees or what he knows? Hitchcock's films of the 30s as realist; his films of the 40s as modernist; and the 50s as postmodernist. Bernardo Bertolucci describing his early films as being like 'sea urchins – very closed, very difficult to handle for an audience'. Isabelle Huppert's comment that *The Piano Teacher* is really about 'the soul of Schubert and the soul of Bach'. Sprites, driads, nymphs, knights, divas, servants, satyrs and statues in Matthew Barney's *Cremaster* series. The conscience of the main character in *Young Adam* is pricked, but fails to bleed. The manner in which Emily Mortimer falls into the canal in *Young Adam*. George Sluizer's *The Vanishing* as the greatest film Krzysztof Kieślowski never made. The idea that *Lost in Translation* is made up of the bits of film that other filmmakers would have left on the cutting room floor. The apartment in *Uzak*. The jump cuts and upside-down shots in *Elizabeth*. Temps mort in Antonioni's films. Barthes' comment that Antonioni's films are 'matte'. The 'exchange of guilt' at the end of Chabrol's *Le Boucher*. The careers of Sally Potter and Paul Cox. The first seven minutes of Kieślowski's *Blue*. Sigourney Weaver's loneliness in *The Ice Storm*. The beginning of *Le Mepris*. The otherworldliness of Michael Powell's *I Know Where I'm Going*. Steve McQueen's coldness in Peckinpah's *The Getaway*. Steve McQueen as the coolest actor in cinema. The fact that the people have shadows in *Last Year in Marienbad*, but not the topiaried shrubs. The match game in *Last Year in Marienbad*. The directness of treatment in Resnais' *Night and Fog*. Frederic Forrest's performance in *Hammett* versus Jason Robard's in *Julia*. The ending of *Les Diaboliques* – the best twist ever? The line 'Match me, Sidney', in Alexander Mackendrick's *Sweet Smell of Success*. Miles Davis' score for Louis Malle's *Lift to the Scaffold*. Erik Satie's "Gymnopédies" in Malle's *Le Feu follet*. Malle's comment that his best films are *Au revoir les enfants*, *Lacombe, Lucien* and *Le Feu follet*, but that his favourite films are *Zazie dans le Métro, Le Souffle au coeur* and *Atlantic City*. The candy-coloured photography in Harmony Korine's *Gummo*. The tilted video camera in *Henry: Portrait of a Serial Killer*. The dialogue between father-in-law and daughter-in-law in Bergman's *Wild Strawberries*. The medieval world portrayed in Bergman's *The Seventh Seal*. The future world portrayed in *Blade Runner*. The chilling opening kidnapping sequence in Sidney Lumet's *Murder on the Orient Express*. The taut, spiralling plot of *No Way Out*. Although it's full of holes, the ingenious plotting for *Memento*. Jack Lemmon's performance in *Missing*. Klaus Maria Brandeur's performance in *Mephisto*. The glowing glass of milk in *Suspicion*. The cut from the scream to the train whistle in Hitchcock's *The 39 Steps*. The missing half-finger in *The 39 Steps*. The car chase in *French Connection* – even better than the one in *Bullitt*? Gene Hackman chasing the boat at the end of *French Connection II*. Gene Hackman playing sax in his wrecked apartment in Coppola's *The Conversation*. Warren Beatty's final run to the open door in *The Parallax View*. The way the paths of Jeff Bridges and Stacy Keach keep crossing in *Fat City*. The money in Addie's hat in *Paper Moon*. The rococo dialogue in Abraham Polonsky's *Force of Evil*. The windscreen wipers and fade to white at the end of *The Unbearable Lightness of Being*.

ABOUT DRY GRASSES BY NURI BILGE CEYLAN

I'M a huge fan and deep admirer of Nuri Bilge Ceylan. I've seen almost all of his movies and love, in particular, *Uzak* and *Once Upon a Time in Anatolia*. For me, that latter movie is a modern masterpiece, but I think he went off the boil a bit since then (2012). I just saw this, his latest, today and it made such an impression on me that I want to get my scattershot thoughts down. In many ways, it's a typical Ceylan movie, about ordinary downtrodden people – in this case a secondary school teacher – bemoaning their lot in life. It's set in a very snowy rural village (snow is a running theme in his movies but you really feel the cold in this one). The initial story is about a complaint of inappropriate behaviour brought against the teacher by one of his pupils. This is in revenge for something the teacher did that involved that student. The film begins in the middle of things so we never really know what has gone on between the two of them, but it's clear they are much more friendly than a teacher and a 14-year old pupil should be. The scenes in which the teacher learns more and more about what has gone on against him behind his back are very tense. The other story is about a woman, Nuray, who is set up on a blind date with the teacher. Some years before, she was involved in a terrorist attack and lost her leg. Her prosthetic is highly advanced and, she says, costs about the same as a mid-range car. She is (not because of that) passionate, direct, and a realist. She's also a left-wing activist. The centrepiece of the movie is a dinner scene between these two. In a 3.5 hour movie, this scene alone is 30 minutes long. It's an absolute tour de force. They talk about everything from social responsibility, the disconnect between thought and action, one's political imperative in life, god. The whole scene is a novel in itself (and there is an eye-popping moment here when Ceylan takes the film into a completely unexpected direction). These two storylines flip-flop and the teacher is put into a couple of very tense, revealing situations, from which he doesn't emerge very well. He's a rebel, not a revolutionary. He's a chancer, choosing to say what he thinks people want to hear rather than how he actually feels. In the film's coda (no spoilers, don't worry), he addresses in an imaginative way the young student who besmirched him, leaving the movie hanging on a highly mysterious, profound cliff. Ceylan is deeply influenced by two Russians – Chekhov and Tarkovsky. His films are a perfect marriage of the two. *About Dry Grasses* is an absolute wonder.

SECRETS OF THE UNIVERSE IN *REMAIN IN LIGHT*

I forgot all my sorrow and started to sing the earthy songs which sorrow prevented me from singing about.

— from *My Life in the Bush of Ghosts*

When people speak passionately, they speak in melodies.

— Brian Eno

The world isn't logical. It's a song.

— David Byrne

I want to start this essay on *Remain in Light* with the impact the singles "Cities" and, especially, "Once in a Lifetime" had on me as an impressionable 15-year-old at comprehensive school in southern England. My school friends and I were a bit too young for punk – I was 11 in 1976 – so it was the New Wave of bands that followed on the heels of punk that we were listening to: The Police, The Jam, The Stranglers, The Clash, The Specials, as well as less cool bands that we wouldn't admit to listening to, but secretly did: Ian Dury & the Blockheads, Blondie, Roxy Music, Dire Straits, The Pretenders. But we all knew how awful bands like Abba and Baccara were and never listened to them – we left that to our parents. Weirdly, none of my friends or I were really into Joy Division. Maybe their music was more suited to the post-industrial landscapes of northern England than rural Sussex, but it was also a question of availability – you just couldn't get hold of Joy Division records in Mastersound, Haywards Heath.

In any case, one night on Top of the Pops in February 1981, I 'witnessed' the video to "Once in a Lifetime". I had never seen anything like it before. Who was this guy who looked like Norman Bates and what was he doing with his body? What was he singing about? He looked so nerdy and mental. I was suspicious and confused about what I had seen, but privately I also felt a strange sense of elation and connection. Much later, I learned more about the song, that he took all the lyrics from TV evangelist shows, for example, and that those jerky hand and body movements were actually taken from African tribal dances. Suddenly, I saw artistry and imagination. Singles were affordable in those days but albums were expensive, and I couldn't afford the album, so that was that. But then serendipity came into play when a school friend, who had bought *Remain in Light* and freaked out at its weirdness, offered to sell it to me half-price. I took the plunge. Listening to the whole album I wasn't quite sure what I was letting myself in for. I was captivated and confused in equal measure and it took me many years to get fully to grips with these songs. The album is a very intense listening experience. The lyrics are clever and oblique, dealing with materialism, information, obsession, confusion, physiognomy, identity, ecology, terrorism, the apocalypse. The music is incredibly manic, drawing heavily on scratch, funk, Fela Kuti's Afro-beat and juju rhythms. Each song is driven by a fast, minimal, pulsating rhythm and the whole thing is torn through by Adrian Belew's screaming banshee guitar.

Of course, all this went right over my head as a 15-year-old, but I was hooked. Looking back now, I can see that *Remain in Light* (along with David Sylvian's *Brilliant Trees*, released just four years later) was one of those pieces of art that changed me forever. First it blew, and then expanded, my mind. It showed me the way forward in life: I was not to be afraid to 'play', to experiment; I should always look for new forms and move forward; I shouldn't worry what anyone else thought; there was no need to conform. I didn't know it then, but *Remain in Light* forged the way forward for me throughout the rest of my life to find ways of accessing my own creativity.

Although *Remain in Light* was Talking Heads' fourth album, it might as well have been their first, so different was it from what came before. It's often been said (did David Bowie say this first?) that there is always one song on an album that points the way forward for the next, and that song for *Remain in Light* was *Fear Of Music*'s 'Life During Wartime', which was born out of the band jamming together at a Detroit sound check. On previous albums, David Byrne had come to the studio with songs already written but, when the band reconvened in the Bahamas to make their fourth album, they decided to carry that process on and build an entire album that way. 'We'd record two and a half, three minutes of groove, and then through editing we'd expand it to, say, five minutes,' Byrne said.

Talking Heads more or less made three kinds of song: those with a hook, those with a mood and/or those with a groove. "Psycho Killer", for example, might have fairly 'dark' subject matter, but it doesn't have a particularly 'dark' mood; in fact, it is quite light and 'poppy'. What it has is a hook: "Fa fa fa fa fa fa fa fa fa fa". "Take Me to the River", by contrast, is not very 'hooky', but it has a massive groove and it is this groove that people respond to when they hear the song. How do the songs on *Remain in Light* fit in with this theory? If we were to draw a Venn diagram of hook, mood and groove, which of the songs would fall right in the middle? Almost all of the songs on *Remain in Light* fall right in the middle, which is one of the reasons it is such a magnificent work of art. However, although the music on *Remain in Light* is obviously remarkable and extraordinary, what I find equally remarkable and extraordinary are the lyrics, an aspect of the album that has hitherto not really been discussed in any great detail.

In the early years of Talking Heads, Byrne drew from all sorts of things for his lyrics – systems theory, cybernetics, conceptual art and, of course, architecture. To the angular, jerky music, Byrne wrote lyrics that were presentations of dysfunctional kooks out of synch in their social environments. Oddballs, misfits, malcontents. The songs were transcriptions of their conversations or inner monologues. He wrote from all sorts of different viewpoints, contradictory or otherwise, none of them to be trusted at all. The most famous 'character' point of view Byrne wrote from is, of course, the psychopath in "Psycho Killer" ('Better run run run run run run run away!'), but there are others. There is the 'spy' in "Life During Wartime". Is 'spy' the right word though? These days, 'urban terrorist' might be a better term. The song is written from the point of view of an urban terrorist, but not from the point of view of their politics, but about the difficulties of their daily life. Then there is the civil servant on "Don't Worry About the Government", who sings happily about his apartment block. Is it sincere, or ironic? Who knows. The man on "Warning Sign" who sings, "Hear my voice, hear my voice/It's saying something, and it's not very nice". The solipsist who casts a disparaging eye over the US and his fellow citizens in "The Big Country". The song "No Compassion" is about exactly that, about a narrator who says, "Compassion is a virtue, but I don't have the time". The man in "New Feeling", who is on the verge of a nervous breakdown (aren't they all?) – "I go visiting, I talk loud/try to make myself clear". "New Feeling" is a narrative that bears an awful lot of similarities with Travis Bickle's story in *Taxi Driver*, which hit the screens just a year before the song was released. Of these early songs, David Byrne himself has said, 'The early songs are, it now seems to me, the work of a fairly disturbed mind – my own – that was using this writing and performance to find out how to be in the world. They appear to be ravings produced by someone in an altered state.'

The lyrics on the first three Talking Heads albums were a gradual refinement of these characters and sensibilities, but *Remain in Light* is a totally different beast. For this album, as well as a whole new approach to the making of the music, Byrne had to abandon his previous experiments with songs, stories and roles and adopt a whole new approach to the lyrics, too.

By way of showing how he did this, I'll refer to Isiah Berlin's famous 1953 essay "The Hedgehog and the Fox". In his essay, Berlin divided writers and thinkers into two categories: hedgehogs – who view the world through the lens of a single defining idea – and foxes, who draw on a wide variety of experiences and for whom the world cannot be boiled down to a single idea. As examples of hedgehogs, Berlin cites Dostoyevsky and Marcel Proust; whereas Aristotle and Shakespeare are foxes. Although Berlin never meant for his essay to be taken at all seriously, its central idea is fascinating and you can see what he means. Basically, Dostoyevsky wrote the same book over and over, as did Proust. Pick up and open *The Devils* or *The Gambler* anywhere and the themes in them are not that dissimilar. But pick up Aristotle's book on ethics, *The Nicomachean Ethics*, and you get something completely different from his book on poetics, *Ars Poetica*. Same goes for Shakespeare – *A Midsummer Night's Dream* is way different to *King Lear*. Aristotle and Shakespeare wrote about many different things, ideas, emotions, philosophies, but we can accurately summarise Dostoevsky's entire output as paving the way for the idea of Existentialism, and that Proust's central concern in his one book was the nature of time and its passage.

On an album like *Fear of Music*, the songs are very different from each other. The existential panic in "Drugs", for instance, is completely unlike the tongue-in-cheek disco of "Cities". The uptight funk of "I Zimbra" is very different in feel to the wistful, melancholic "Heaven". The songs on *Fear of Music* are foxes, for sure. The songs on *Remain in Light*, however, are hedgehogs – they are of a piece, cut from the same cloth. Rather than use conventional lyrics based on a social misfit's view of the world, the words of the songs of *Remain in Light* are collages, drawn directly from TV evangelists, Southern preachers, *New York Post* headlines, the Watergate tapes, the testimonies of former slaves and those African texts Byrne had studied with Brian Eno. The lyrics are still written from a character's point of view, but the character's role is now more like an omniscient narrator, an Everyman. You and me.

On "Once in a Lifetime", in particular, David Byrne is in character as a suburban man who becomes, in a moment of insight, a kind of post-modern preacher, asking himself (and us) a series of questions that he doesn't have answers to, questions for us to consider and ask ourselves about our lives. In this guise of declamatory preacher dismantling the American Dream, Byrne contrasted the transitory nature of desire and acquisition with the permanence of the elements, with choruses soaring out of a tugging undercurrent of percussion. Its final refrain, assuring the listener of life continuing in a state of nature, 'same as it ever was,' was like a forceful, purgative exhalation of breath following years of holding back. Talking about the narrator of "Once in a Lifetime", Byrne says, 'He's not upset or tormented, just bewildered.'

This time round, Byrne was drawing more on other people's life experiences, news stories, testimonies and less on cybernetics or systems theory. The lyrics are clever and oblique and, although they still deal with 'difficult' themes, the results seem warmer than before, more inclusive, universal. Of this process, Byrne says, 'I have definite ideas about which phrase is right for a line and which is not, but I couldn't tell why. Some of my choices don't make sense in any logical way. I just have an intuitive sense about them.'

But – and here's the key – in addition to this new approach to the main vocal, using collage rather than character study, *Remain in Light* contains a secret weapon – its backing vocals. It is the use of backing vocals on the album that gives it the weight of truth, the veracity of human experience. They act as a Greek chorus, offering an alternative commentary to the main narrator. My contention is that, taken together, the vocals and backing vocals on *Remain in Light* contain nothing other than the secrets of the universe and, making such a huge claim, I'd like to look in some detail at how the backing vocals work.

Each song begins with Byrne singing (or intoning) the single main vocal – the 'point' – in either first-person point of view ("Born under Punches"/"Crosseyed and Painless"/"Once in a Lifetime"/"Houses in Motion"/"The Overload"), close third ("Seen and Not Seen"/"Listening Wind") or as an omniscient narrator ("The Great Curve"), but, whatever point of view is used, it is always a single voice up, close and personal, not distant or impersonal. The singer/speaker is always relaying to the listener something of great personal importance and significance. The tone is urgent.

In conventional rock, pop, soul (or whatever) music, backing vocals are nearly always used to repeat a phrase or line of the main vocal in order to to emphasise its thematic importance, or its hook, or perhaps the backing vocals come in to join the main vocalist in the chorus, to bulk it up and make it more catchy. In whichever way they are used, it is nearly always in support of the lead singer. The backing vocals on *Remain in Light* are not used like that at all. When the multi-tracked backing vocals come into a song on *Remain in Light*, they are independent of the main vocals. They offer no support; indeed they are there to contradict, or offer an alternative to, the 'point' of the main vocal. In this way, they are the 'counterpoint' to the main vocal, its antiphon, a response to the main vocal's call. They carry equal weight and importance as the main vocal, giving it balance and a broader perspective.

This balance is also carried in its tone. Whereas the main vocal line is urgent, pressing, the backing vocals take a much smoother, softer line. They explain, reassure, calm. They seem to be more knowledgeable than the main singer/speaker; they seem to possess a much greater understanding of the existential uncertainty or skepticism conveyed in the main vocal. Indeed, it is left to the 'voice of reason' of the backing vocals to express clearly the most complicated ideas – the secrets of the universe – in each of the tracks on *Remain in Light*.

The main vocal line and the backing vocals in every song on *Remain in Light* (with the exception of "The Overload") work in this way, operating and interlocking together to offer a psychic wholeness that neither could achieve on its own. The two vocal lines move alone, together, coming in and out, like ballet dancers, allowing each to move independently, yet, by their very proximity, their symbiosis, offering a joint perspective, so that there is always a 'compare and contrast' going on in the listener's mind. Without one of these lines, you would not be able to fully appreciate the other.

This process is taken to its apogee on *Remain in Light* on "The Great Curve", where, in contrast to the main vocal, there are three backing vocal lines, each with a distinct melody, layering and weaving their words into endless circular patterns, so that, taken together, they offer a communal, spiritual, 'total' vision of humanity's at-one-ness with Gaia, or Mother Earth. The ideas contained within these backing vocal lines are sublime in the true sense of the word, i.e. that they present ideas and images that are too great to be fully understood by a single human being's consciousness. Byrne says, 'Almost all the vocals we put on it have to do with one kind of religious experience or another.' The way these antiphonal backing vocals are used on the album give it a profundity never before (or since) encountered on a 'rock' record and they remain unique to *Remain in Light*.

PRIDE BY ROBERT PALMER

SADLY, Robert Palmer passed away in 2003 at the shockingly young age of 54 without much comment or celebration, which is a crying shame because he was a massively underrated and largely overlooked artist who wrote and produced so many great songs.

Palmer was born in Yorkshire but grew up in Malta before moving back to the UK as a teenager and this early formative experience led to a peripatetic life which embraced many (world) music styles in his music – soul, rock, blues, reggae, calypso, soca. Starting out in the UK as a rhythm & blues singer, he eventually left Vinegar Joe (which also featured Elkie Brooks) to forge a solo career for himself as a white soul boy, culminating in the terrific album *Double Fun.* Palmer bypassed punk altogether and headed straight to the New Wave on *Looking for Clues*, which contained two classic electro tunes – "Looking for Clues" and "Johnny and Mary". For the following album, *Pride*, he went all-out electro, producing an album that easily stands as his most consistent, entertaining and absorbing piece of work.

Palmer had moved his family to the Bahamas in 1978 and the islands obviously worked their magic on this album, which mixes electronica with Caribbean rhythms to create a sunny, light-hearted feel throughout. Opener, the eponymous "Pride", name checks Oliva Newton-John and is a bizarre anti-exercise rant with an equally bizarre video filmed in a squash court, but its calypso-flavoured hi-stylin' rhythm is irresistible. The off-kilter reggae lilt of "Deadline" is equally catchy, wrong footing the listener with its tricky drum track. The itchy-catchiness continues with the Burundidrum heaviness of "Want You More" and straight-ahead disco of "Dance For Me". The hit single from the album, "You Are in My System", is a masterclass in drum programming that has, unlike most of the gated-drum tracks of the mid '80s, aged pretty well. The only spot on the pristine production and songwriting is a cheesy, sorry cheery, cover version of Kool and the Gang's "You Can Have It". Otherwise, the quality control throughout is kept high, continuing with "Say You Will" and "What You Waiting For".

And then, out of the blue, to close the album off, comes one of the weirdest and most wonderful songs I've ever heard – "The Silver Gun", a five-minute Indian raga sung by Palmer in Urdu. The pulsating polyrhythm of this track is utterly beguiling. God knows what Palmer's singing about but hats off for taking such a huge risk and ending the album on such a wonderfully eccentric note.

Pride did very little on the radio and nothing in the shops. Palmer would go on to much bigger things shortly afterwards with his massive hit "Addicted to Love" and his stint in the short-lived but highly successful Power Station, and then he went back to his roots with a period of recording ballads and blues songs. But, for this listener at least, he had already hit his artistic peak with *Pride*. Not bad for a boy from Batley.

ALTA PLANA BY CHARLIE TATE

WITHOUT any announcement at all, *Alta Plana* appeared in 2005 as a digital-only release and promptly disappeared. I've never met a single person who's heard *of* it, let alone listened to it, but it's one of the most amazingly put together downtempo breakbeat albums I've ever heard.

Each track has an astounding array of ambient detail in it – fireworks, street chatter, trains, a rainstorm, waves, phones ringing, bottles opening, people talking – and is also sublimely produced with crisp, kicking drums, great cymbal-work, sampled piano and strings, electric keyboards and deep-down bass.

The album opener, "Dar el Salam" begins with the sound of a train rolling into a station. Then keys and a mind-bendingly deep bass line kick in and the whole gorgeous thing just takes off.

"Con Chin" is insanely catchy, starting with just shakers and bass, then developing into a very mellow groove based around a sampled conversation between an old man explaining to another man that the food he has to offer is free. It's full of loud birdsong and breaking waves, suggesting a tropical island. Who is Chin? And who is with him? It's a beautiful mystery.

"Inassire (Dub)" circles around the hilarious 'harmonica' speech given by Jason Robards in *Once Upon a Time in the West*. "Don't You Know" is the smoothest track on the album and could well be an outtake by TLC. Other flavours on show are the reggae-ish "Fe Regi" (featuring a sample from Barrington Levy's "Here I Come") and the hip hoppy "Ramsden Road".

When I discovered *Alta Plana*, I tried to track Charlie Tate down. Who was this guy and what else had he produced? Maybe the cover photo would provide a clue? Where was that photo shot?

It was obviously some kind of salt plane. The title *Alta Plana* is Spanish for 'high plane'. Was that important? After a bit of investigation, I worked out that the photo must have been taken on the Uyuni Salt Flat in Bolivia, which is indeed high, nearly 12,000ft high, in fact. That might account for some of the Spanish song titles, like "Por Favor Adolfo" and "Viva San Telmo", although San Telmo is confusingly in Buenos Aires.

Did Charlie Tate live in Bolivia? Or Argentina? Or maybe Dar El Salam (which is in Egypt and not to be confused with Dar Es Salaam, which is in Tanzania)? I've literally spent years trying to find out who or where he is, but have failed miserably.

Not only did the album sink without trace, Charlie Tate seems keen to leave no trace either. Whoever you are, would the real Charlie Tate please stand up and take a bow?

SILVER APPLES OF THE MOON BY LAIKA

The explosion and proliferation of electronic music in the 1990s threw up some incredible acts, many of whom should be much better known than they are. Laika were one such group. Founded in 1993 by American writer/vocalist Margaret Fiedler and British engineer/producer Guy Fixsen, Laika took Jamaican dub techniques and combined them with the motorik of krautrock, adding Rhodes keys, jazzy flutes, vibes and marimbas, to create their lush, textured, unclassifiable sound. Their debut album, *Silver Apples of the Moon*, named after Morton Subotnick's pioneering Buchla workout, arrived out of nowhere in a plain brown cover with Russian stamps and an air mail sticker on it. There was indeed strange fruit inside.

Opener, "Sugar Daddy", emerges out of a cacophony of clattering drums and develops into an insanely catchy rhythm track, the fluttering and pounding of which sounds like an arrhythmic heartbeat. Next up is the incredibly dense "Marimba Song", all repeated marimbas and jittery snares, giving it a vaguely Steve Reich-esque feel. It is highly claustrophobic and very propulsive. The weird whirring noises, overlapping polyrhythmic drums and the heavy dropping bass line of "Coming Down Glass" are a sheer joy to behold, getting the hips moving in its undertow.

"If You Miss" is a contender for Laika's finest five minutes. Marimbas (again), bass and shakers combine in a tightly repetitive pattern that is matched by Fiedler's simple, repeated lyrics – 'Jump at the sun / And if you miss / You can't help but / Grab some stars' – sung as a round, adding to the sense of its infinite cycle (the 12" vinyl version ended in a locked groove).

The key to all this, and all these fine tracks, is bassist John

Frenett – a truly outstanding and woefully under-appreciated low-end expert up there with the likes of Jah Wobble and Derek Forbes. Frenett's signature dub-style approach and Lou Ciccotelli's proto-African beats are the heart of Laika, providing the band with bass energy and rhythmic complexity.

Listening to *Silver Apples of the Moon* today, it's noticeable how well the band avoided falling into the trap of sounding like any of their contemporaries. Where so many bands from the 1990s now sound dated, Laika's tracks remain fresh and utterly original as ever. They lasted 10 years and made four fine albums during that period, but sales eluded them and they split in 2003.

It's a crime they didn't get what they worked so hard for, but at least we have their records. Those few people, in that particular time and place, worked together to create moments of magic.

CANAXIS BY HOLGER CZUKAY & ROLF DAMMERS

IN the pre-internet early '90s, I heard rumours of this album's existence. People spoke about it in hushed tones, as a thing of lost beauty, but copies of the album were rare as hens' teeth and no one seemed to have actually listened to it. Did it really exist or was it just a myth? Then, in the mid '90s, Can started to reissue their back catalogue, including this, in a brand new cover with sleeve notes. Hallelujah! Glowing reviews followed and early champions included Scanner (aka Robin Rimbaud) and Paul Schütze. I eventually got hold of a copy myself but nothing prepared me for what I was about to hear and, safe to say, I've never fully recovered.

Back in 1968, when Can formed, the group's bassist, sound engineer and editor Holger Czukay was still a student of legendary composer Stockhausen. Czukay knew someone with a key to Stockhausen's studio and, at night, Czukay would steal his way in and use his teacher's equipment to make his own work. Czukay said that *Canaxis* took a long time to prepare but only four hours to record, with lines of tape running around beer bottles spread out on the studio floor.

Co-produced with Rolf Dammers, the album comprises two long tracks entitled "Boat-woman-song" and "Canaxis". The two tracks are essentially DIY electroacoustic pieces, combining ethnic samples culled from short wave radio transmissions with electronic textures. The sample on the first track is of two Vietnamese women singing and is taken from *Music of Viet Nam*, an album of field recordings originally released in 1966 by the American Folkways label. The vocals on the second track are not referenced but they sound suspiciously like Tibetan monks to this untrained ear.

Using these found recordings from across Asia, Czukay then manipulated and looped them into slow, trippy, deeply meditative pieces, full of cavernous clangs, bells and gongs, sudden emergences and drops in pitch, all enmeshed in the blips and bleeps of radio frequencies. The highly-repetitive nature of the voices and loops gives the tracks a drone-like quality and the fact that the voices and loops fade very slowly over time creates a disorientating sense of time slipping away. The pieces never really end; they just gradually fade, like a freight train being forever shunted into sidings. Listening to it is a hallucinatory, hypnotic experience.

In his book, *Ocean of Sound*, David Toop described *Canaxis* as being made up of 'impossible musics from unknown worlds'. In this way, Czukay's attention to the spatial quality of the music and his conjuring of voices out of the aether bear a strong similarity to the studio techniques being used by the dub pioneers in Kingston, Jamaica, at around the same time. Indeed, in interview, Czukay referred to Lee Perry as his 'spiritual brother' and you can see why: both men were mavericks who traded in the art of 'magick' and both were as mad as a bag of squirrels. Described as a cross between Friedrich Nietzche and Frank Zappa, Czukay always played the clown but, be careful, he was deadly serious and a master of his craft. Indeed, *Canaxis* shows us that Czukay was in fact a shaman.

The album was recorded more than 10 years before Brian Eno & David Byrne's similar and much better known *My Life in the Bush of Ghosts* and is now acknowledged as one of the first (and finest) examples of 'ambient' and 'world' music. It is a thing of utter purity and beauty. Get hold of a copy yourself and prepare to be transported by those impossible musics from unknown worlds.

BRILLIANT TREES BY DAVID SYLVIAN

WHEN David Bowie died, I was shocked at how strongly and deeply his death affected me. Little did I know, but there had been an invisible influence on me since I clandestinely listened to my older sister's copy of *"Heroes"* when I was 12, an influence that I only became aware of when he was gone. Maybe because I was that much older (19 years old as opposed to 12) when *Brilliant Trees* came out that this wasn't the case at all with David Sylvian. I was old enough to know right from the moment I first heard *Brilliant Trees* that he was an artist, more or less contemporary with me, from whom I could and would take instruction on how to live.

Brilliant Trees:

'Pulling Punches' is basically 'Art of Parties' part two. 'Art of Parties' itself sounded a lot like the Afro-funk experiments on Talking Heads' *Remain in Light*, particularly 'Born Under Punches' (is the mention of 'punches' coincidental? Probably not, given Sylvian's habit of quoting his influences in song titles.)

'The Ink in the Well' is the first real departure for Sylvian from his work with Japan. The jazz basis in its line-up of Danny Thompson and Kenny Wheeler is carried on throughout the rest of his output on *Gone to Earth* and *Secrets of the Beehive*.

'Nostalgia' is another departure from his previous work for him but in a different direction from 'The Ink in the Well'. Far more ambient in its basis, 'Nostalgia' is perhaps named after Tarkovsky's movie of the same name, a film which has the same watery elements as Sylvian's song. 'Nostalgia' was greatly the result of Holger Czukay's involvement and input into the track, especially with his trademark radio frequencies, and its essentially ambient nature would be picked up again and explored further in Sylvian's collaboration with Czukay on *Plight & Premonition*.

It seemed right that 'Red Guitar' was the first single from *Brilliant Trees* as it is Sylvian's call-to-arms, his statement of intent. It clearly states what Sylvian intended to do as an artist from then on. Like, 'The Ink in the Well', it has a jazz basis of piano, bass, drums and its lyrics again reference Sylvian's influences, this time Cocteau's *Devil in the Flesh* and Satre's *Iron in my Soul*.

Side Two of *Brilliant Trees* comprises three tracks (tracks, not songs) but, in reality, it is one long piece of work, such is the flow from one into the other. For me, Side Two of *Brilliant Trees* is the most meaningful side of any album I've ever heard. Steve Jansen's steadfast, 'on it' drum beat in both 'Weathered Wall' and 'Backwaters' provides the backbone that anchors the swirls and eddies of textures created by Holger Czukay's radio frequencies, Jon Hassell's electric trumpet and Ryuichi Sakamoto's synth washes. For the title track, it's just organ and trumpet that provides the shimmering backdrop for the hymn-like exhortation to find one's spiritual roots and therefore one's way in life. The Tao. The voice then drops away and Hassell's trumpet, Jansen's surdo drum and handclaps accompany a long outro of more synth textures that flurry and throb until the track's abrupt end. It's an instrumental section that hints towards the ethnic environment conveyed in the subsequent *Words with the Shaman* EP that Sylvian, Czukay and Hassell collaborated again on. Taken together, these three tracks form a triptych of artistic purpose, a manifesto by Sylvian to find the deep sources inside oneself, to tap them and let creative life flow from them. I, for one, took heed.

GREEN BY R.E.M.

FOR me, this is their strongest album – it starts powerfully and doesn't let up throughout in terms of intensity or quality. Its perfectly symmetrical structure – 2-1-2-1-2-1-2 – is two fast rock songs followed by a slow ballad, ending on the uplifting hidden final track. Kicking off with the generically-titled 'Pop Song 89', with its killer angular riff, who would follow such a fast and furious rock song with the even faster, breathless imperative of 'Get Up'? The music boxes in the bridge are a moment of magic. Then we get the yearning, plaintive 'You Are Everything', the first of three Southern Gothic ballads on the album, all gorgeous gems featuring Peter Buck's mandolin for the first time. Then we get 'Stand', with its insanely catchy riff – apparently a dumb goofball pop song, but actually a bit more meaningful than it pretends to be. Was there ever a song as politically prescient as 'World Leader Pretend'? It could have been written for Trump. I remember Stipe performing this song on the Green World Tour with so much passion, banging a chair with a metal rod and singing through a megaphone. The Air side closes with the incredibly moving 'The Wrong Child' and the Metal side opens with one of the absolute jewels in REM's crown, 'Orange Crush', with yet another granular, catchy guitar riff. 'Turn You Inside-Out' is REM at their downright meanest and moodiest – a monster track and one of their best deep cuts. The delicate, luminous 'Hairshirt' never fails to move with its confessional... Another often-overlooked track in REM's back catalogue is 'I Remember California', which features some more amazing angular guitar work from Buck. The whole thing is wrapped up with the final 'hidden' track, referred to as 'The Eleventh Untitled Song', which has a naive, child-like feel to it due to the group's swapping of instruments. This song starts the trend of the band ending their albums on an enigmatic yet hopeful note ('Me In Honey', 'Find The River'). Overall, there are so many things that make this album so strong – Mike Mills' harmonies, with their often contradictory lines ('complicate/complement'), the even production which gives the album a consistent tone, Buck's guitar and mandolin playing, the gothic-ness, the clear melodies... I must have listened to this album a thousand times and I still find so much depth in it.

'HOW DOES THAT OLD SONG GO?'
DESERTER'S SONGS AT 25

Bands, those funny little plans, that never work quite right.
— "Holes"

IN the mid 1990s, Jonathan Donahue was at the lowest point in his life. Sales of Mercury Rev's last album *See You on the Other Side* (1995) had been terrible, the tour to promote it had been ill attended and gruelling and the band were in huge debt and in disarray. After three albums and years of touring, the group split and went their separate ways. Penniless, Donahue retreated to a cabin in the Catskill Mountains to lick his wounds. It was back to square one. During this time, Donahue began listening again to some of the records he used to listen to as a child, including a collection of spoken word fairytales set to classical music. Inspired by these pieces, he started to compose simple melodies on the piano.

Meanwhile, in a Jesuit monastery in upstate New York, Mercury Rev co-founder and guitarist, Grasshopper, was in retreat. Immediately after finishing the disastrous tour for *See You on the Other Side,* Grasshopper ended up there to dry out and clear his head. 'It was a very clearing experience and it might've been a catalyst to paring down the music. After I came out I'd developed this Zen thing of not playing all the time, just playing in the spots,' Grasshopper has said. Unbeknownst to either of them at the time, these new paths being taken separately by Donahue and Grasshopper would eventually lead to *Deserter's Songs*.

Before that, though, something happened to Donahue that was the spark. In 1997, he received a phone call out of the blue from the Chemical Brothers. They were big fans of Mercury Rev and would Donahue like to work with them on a track? Donahue couldn't believe what he was hearing. He had thought that no one was interested in Mercury Rev and to get that kind of endorsement from such a popular and successful band rekindled something in Donahue that had long been dead. 'Sure!' he said. The nine and a half minute track, "Private Psychedelic Reel", was the result and appeared on the group's 1997 album, *Dig Your Own Hole*. It had done the trick and Donahue was up and working again. He got back in touch with Grasshopper and played some early demos to him. Liking what he heard, Grasshopper joined Donahue in the Catskills and the pair began work on the songs that would make up the album.

During this time, at the local hardware store, Donahue kept on seeing two of The Band's original members, organist Garth Hudson and drummer Levon Helm, both of whom lived in the area. While touring *See You On The Other Side*, Mercury Rev had begun to work cover versions by The Band into the set. 'We do love The Band,' Donahue says, 'so one day I just went up to them and said, "We're a band you've never heard of and we've got some peculiar songs, would you like to come on over and play on them?" They said, "Sure!".' In the end, Helm ended up playing drums on "Opus 40" while Hudson contributed alto and tenor sax to "Hudson Line". 'On *Deserter's Songs* we took a lot of inspiration from their music,' Donahue admits. 'You can hear that it's pretty direct. We like the way they carry themselves as people and the honesty and sincerity that goes into some of their music. That's the sort of destination you look towards for yourself, just to do it sincerely and not worry about what people think. They were one of the few bands we had a lot in common with.'

Deserter's Songs opens with the magnificent "Holes". Strings fade in, a spacey Wurlitzer swirls, and Donahue's keening falsetto sings, "Time, all the long red lines, that take control…" Then an acoustic guitar and drums kick in. A bowed saw warbles in the background. The stately "Tonight it Shows" follows with its distinct Brian Wilson-esque pizzicato strings and piccolos. The warm melancholic mood is carried on in the woodwind instruments, picked acoustic guitar and female soprano backing vocals of third track "Endlessly". Listening to the instrumental versions of these first three tracks, you'd be forgiven for thinking you were listening to late Rachmaninov. It's brave to start any album with a track as slow and otherworldly as "Holes", but to follow it with, not one, but two equally mid tempo, mainly acoustic, quasi-classical tracks like "Tonight It Shows" and "Endlessly" is a truly audacious statement of intent.

We're back on more familiar territory with fourth track "Opus 40". Opening with sampled strings and Hammond organ locked into a loop together, the song is a hazy, psychedelic, epic adventure, beginning with the image of a woman "climbing from the suicide machine". Side One closes with Grasshopper's contribution to the album, "The Hudson Line", a simple lullaby about escaping New York City to the Catskills on the railway line that follows the Hudson River, just as Grasshopper had done to make *Deserter's Songs*.

Side Two begins with "Goddess on a Hiway" a tune by Donahue that had been lying around since the late '80s and which Grasshopper had to convince Donahue to resurrect. Good decision. This gorgeous power pop song was the first hugely successful single from the album. Like "Opus 40", the next track, "The Funny Bird", is another beautifully psychedelic and enigmatic song: "like the way along the coast, I've come to love the highs and lows". I have poured over the lyrics to this song and listened to it hundreds of times and it is still as inscrutable as ever. It's my personal favourite from the album, a brilliant, intense statement.

The album closes with the celebratory, kick-ass "Delta Sun Bottleneck Stomp" and 'stomp' is the right word. The song is a marching band doing Mardi Gras. The track is a collaboration with the Chemical Brothers, whom Donahue had invited to return the favour.

Although there are 11 songs listed, there are only actually eight songs on the record. The other three tracks are 'cinematic' interludes, not so much songs as scenes from old scratchy, 8mm movies with soundtracks of drones, organs, bowed saws and hammered upright piano. They punctuate the album beautifully. There is a strong cinematic feel to the whole album. Mercury Rev kind of started out as filmmakers before falling into making music. Grasshopper and Donahue first met while attending the State University of New York at Buffalo. Under the tutelage of the famous minimalist composer, Tony Conrad, Grasshopper was making short films and invited Donahue to write and perform music to accompany them. 'Conrad was working in the Media Studies department then,' Grasshopper remembers. 'Although he was supposed to be teaching video he would also talk about film, music and performance art. The man knows everything. He talked a lot about his influences, John Cage, Edgard Varèse, Erik Satie and Henry Cowell, all of which were new to me. I would go out and buy the records and play them to Jonathan.'

The visual aspect is also dominant in the lyrics for *Deserter's Songs*. A motif of 'eyes' runs through the album. Eyes, the 'newness' of seeing, correcting vision or destroying it, all this adds to the child-like wonder of the songs:

"Angry jealous spies/Got telephones for eyes" ("Holes")
"An th' darkships of her eyes/Surrender t' you suddenly"("Endlessly")

"And slamming her eyes, locking the door/She collapses down upon the ocean floor" ("Opus 40")

"When I see your eyes arrive/They explode like two bugs on glass" ("Goddess on a Hiway")

"Have your eyes all been destroyed?" ("The Funny Bird")

The band leaked a few of the tracks to the Chemical Brothers back in the UK, who raved about them to anyone who would listen. They knew that something very special was happening. Eventually, a British record company, V2, got hold of the tapes and agreed to fund the rest of the album. This meant that the band could use producer, original member and bass player Dave Fridmann's expensive studio and, over a period of two months, all the string parts and wind instruments were recorded. *Deserter's Songs* was released on 29th September 1998. No one expected it to do anything but word-of-mouth quickly spread, particularly in the UK, where the album sold well and was eventually named Album of the Year by NME and other music magazines.

A few years after its release. I happened to see an art exhibition called 'American Gothic', a collection of paintings made in the 1800s of the vast American landscapes. As I stood looking at those paintings of the snowy peaks, the planes and great rivers of the midwest, I understood for the first time, really, the epic nature that Donahue and co had managed to capture on songs like the widescreen "Goddess on a Hiway", the cosmic nature of "Holes" or the god's-eye view of "Opus 40".

Deserter's Songs was the album Mercury Rev were always destined to make. The experiences of disappointment and loss brought a softness and maturity to Mercury Rev's sound. Previously, the band had been a meeting place for Pharoah Sanders, The Allman Brothers and Harry Partch, with added layers of fuzz and feedback, and you can still hear traces of that in "Opus 40" and "The Funny

Bird", but *Deserter's Songs* is a wholly different kind of prospect, a whole different level of sophistication and elegance. I can't think of many other such drastic changes in direction that a band has taken in modern guitar/rock music. Maybe Johnny Cash with his American Recordings series. Maybe. Donahue has said that playing in the early days of Mercury Rev was like being in the middle of a whirlpool, but the waters of *Deserter's Songs* are calmer, and deeper. It's an album made by a band with nothing more to lose. They made it thinking that no one would hear it except themselves. It was supposed to be their valediction. On its surprising success, Donahue says, 'It had the feeling of rebirth, of going down to the grave for quite a while and lying down there in the darkness and the quiet, and then someone pulls you up and shakes the dirt off you and says "No, you thought you were dead, but you're not"'.

The album has one last trick up its sleeve. As the last glorious final notes of "Delta Sun Bottleneck Stomp" fade out and you think the whole thing is over, some moments pass and then a hidden track begins – snippets of staccato strings, very spiky and strident, and percussion. It sounds like a classical piece written by Edgard Varèse (whose work also reflected the magnitude of the American landscape). It's a complete surprise. Then, in amongst the intense strings, there is the sound of a man calling, like a sailor on the brow of a ship calling into the sea fog to see if anyone is there, a lone voice in the vastness. It's an apt closing image to the album – the good ship Mercury Rev and all who sail in her floating off into the unknown.

MOUSE ON MARS – A PRIMER

FRANÇOIS

Truffaut believed that you could sum up an entire movie in one word – his word for *Last Year in Marienbad* was 'persuasion' – and if there is one word that sums up Mouse on Mars' career thus far, I would suggest the word 'playfulness'. They have never been as 'challenging' as the concrete analog noise of Panasonic or Main, nor as predictable as the made-to-order electronica for the club generation (Chemical Brothers anyone?) – instead, they have spent the last 21 years seeking to challenge themselves and their audience at every turn by playful exploration while, at the same time, miraculously managing not to descend into pedantic exercises or pointless noodling.

For a long time, the myth was that Jan St Werner and Andi Toma met in the early 90s at a death metal concert. The truth turns out to be a little more prosaic – they actually met in the audience of a rock contest at Cologne's Popkomm trade fair. They quickly formed a very close working relationship and fell easily in line with each other's thinking – they even sign themselves 'Jandi'. 'It's something very intimate, you can't do music with anyone,' says St Werner. Their very first recording together resulted in the single "Frosch" (frog in German), released in 1994, and people immediately tagged them with the Ambient Techno label alongside acts such as Higher Intelligence Agency, Aphex Twin, Spacetime Continuum and Orbital. However, they quickly shook off that label and moved onto pastures new. Of those early ambient/electonica outfits, few remain, and their only contemporaries (as a duo) to have built an equally solid body of work and to have kept their reputation similarly intact are Autechre and Plaid.

Looking back over their career, they do seem to have more fun than most, which must derive from the fact that Mouse on Mars have always deliberately and systematically avoided being lumped into any school of thought, trend or movement. They shun linear progression, preferring instead to sidestep any second guessing by producing each time something completely different from the time before. The one consistent element in their career is their non-consistency. In 1998, Andi Toma explained, 'We don't feel part of any electronic movement, or any other movement. In fact, we have just three synthesisers and two samplers, so most guitar bands are actually more electronic than we are. In the future, things will be more interesting with electronic music because there will be better computers, but if you work with computers, you have to work harder to make sure the music isn't just code. We want to make it more organic – we see our music as a community of sounds, and we make sure the sound has a position in the music.'

This is a pretty good summary, and manifesto, for their entire output to date. Words like 'community' and 'society' have figured prominently in their thinking and approach to their work since they began making music and this sense of openness reached its apogee in 2014 with the release of *21 Again*, a set of collaborations with friends and fellow musicians to celebrate their first 21 years of making music. To coin a phrase, the Future Is Now, and so to see whether or not Andi Toma's prediction that things will be more interesting with electronic music because there will be better computers has come true, this seems like a good time to assess their journey up to and including their latest release *21 Again*.

Vulvaland

Too Pure CD 1994

Iaora Tahiti

Too Pure CD 1995

Their debut album, *Vulvaland*, is by far Mouse on Mars' most focussed effort. These early tracks were a digital coming together of three strains of music: the kinetic four-to-the-floor techno of "Frosch" (based on a sample from Iggy Pop's *Zombie Birdhouse* album), the dub of Prince Far-I on "Future Dub" and the Krautrock of Can and Neu! on "Katang". Aside from the abrasiveness of that 29-minute closing track, the rest of the album is a collection of blissed-out ambient 4/4 grooves, which isn't surprising as it was released on the last waves of music produced by Generation E. 20 years later, it still sounds pretty damn good.

Much more structured was the distressed textures and digital cut-and-paste IDM of *Iaora Tahiti*, which is a contender for their most accomplished piece of work to date. Opening track "Stereomission" has a stifling bassline as the undertow, hooking and pulling us through the candy-coloured pop, but the digital surface is notched, punctured and chinked, revealing the dub effects hidden deep inside, sloshing around like soup. "Schlecktron" is one of the heaviest tracks Mouse on Mars have ever produced – the sound of a spacecraft emitting distress signals from above the seething, swirling surface of a red-hot planet. And then there's the incredible "Bib", with its ghostly choir intoning over the shimmering percussive rush – Mouse on Mars' first negotiation with the blind joy that is Jungle. The Rousseau-esque "Papa, Antoine" was positively tropical with its use of kiddy roto toms, oompah bass and pedal steel guitar and the whole thing signs off with the beautiful, wistful "Hallo", a claustrophobic listening experience, like being trapped inside a large multi-coloured balloon.

Glam

Sonig CD 1998

In the mid-'90s, Mouse on Mars were called upon for a couple of head-scratching projects. One was to produce an album for Kraftwerk's Wolfgang Flür (of which more later); the other was a commission from Hollywood producer George Edmunds (son of Ali McGraw) to record the soundtrack for a B-movie entitled *Gangster Glam*, directed by ex-boxer and actor Tony Danza. Toma and St Werner duly took up the offer: 'We synced the video to the instruments, so the video tape was leading the computer. It has a different personality. We would never have done it that way if it had been music for music's sake.' The producers were completely baffled by what MoM came up with and rejected it on the grounds that it was too 'uncommercial'. Initially, Toma and St Werner disowned the project and it looked destined never to be heard, but MoM thought better of it and, when they parted company with Too Pure after the *Iaora Tahiti* album, they decided to set up their own record company, Sonig, one of whose first releases was *Glam*. Thank goodness they did, because the album is unlike anything else in their oeuvre and, after nearly 20 years, still sounds current and relevant.

The opening track, "Port Dusk", begins with three minutes of warm fuzz, billowing in and out of the speakers before we get a grinding crunch of clattering beats, a power drill bursting into a lava lamp. These harsh metallic tones continue on the aptly-named "Grindscore" before evolving into the flurry of the butterfly beats of "Snap Bar". The rumbling cinematic moodiness continues over a further 12 tracks with titles such as "Mood Leck Backlash", "Tiplet Metal Plate" and "Heizchase Nailway". Indeed, *Glam* exemplifies just as well as any MoM album the fantastic wordplay in their titles, which recall and echo recognisable nouns and syntax but are always off-kilter with their own pre-lingual inventions. Again, 'playful' is the word. The cold presses of clicks, whirrs and burrs of sound here is as close to Isolationist drifts and drones as MoM ever got. Track after track conjures images of blasted, crepuscular landscapes and icy climates, cold and forbidding, all filtered through a dubby fluid undercurrent. This is a seriously accomplished piece of work, which (like all great art) was met by bafflement and indifference on its release, but which sounds better and better as the years go by.

Instrumentals

Domino CD 2000

Rost Pocks

Too Pure CD 2003

Back in '95/'96, MoM were producing incredible tracks that made fantastic use of dub effects, but it was many years before these early vinyl-only compilation singles and EPs were re-released as CD collections. The first of these, *Instrumentals*, is made up of various compilation tracks from that period and about half of them are among the finest that Mouse on Mars have recorded. "Pegel Gesetzt" begins with a slow build up of static and bass before evolving into a softly patterned children's lullaby. "Owai" is straight-ahead, no nonsense techno, driven by sten-gun bass and leviathan belches. The stray whips and cracks of sound in "Subnubus" (featured on the compilation *Folds And Rhizomes For Gilles Deleuze*) are the perfect embodiment of Deleuze's rhizomes – strands of sound that grow in an organic, vegetal way, finding growth and renewal in, and through, the gaps of a song. "Chromantic" is Mouse on Mars at their softest and warmest – the gorgeous melody line is subtle and wistful, and the whole thing is earthed by its very liquid bassline. Best of all is "Rompatroullie" with its nod to the Peter Thomas Sound Orchestra. The dancehall-reggae dub effects on this track are outstandingly used to create depth and breadth in sound, and the push-pull, stop-start rhythm is absolutely beguiling.

Rost Pocks collects together the EPs *Frosch*, *Bib*, *Cache Cœur Naïf* and *Twift* and the "Saturday Night Worldcup Fieber" 12" single on one glorious CD and, although you might think it's for completists only, it is actually a good place to start the wonderful Mouse on Mars adventure in sound. Things kick off with "Frosch" and end with its kissing cousin, "Froschroom", a longer, loopier version. In between sit some of the most gorgeous electronic music you're ever likely to hear: the glorious kick-ass Krautrock of "Schnee Bud" from the *Frosch* EP, the sublime "Maus Mobil", with its post-breakbeat push-pull and Jah Wobbley bassline, the wiggly Fruit mix of "Saturday Night" – a breathtaking example of mid-'90s breakbeat mayhem being applied to the gloss of minutely-programmed and precise rhythms to produce a track with squishy depth. On a lighter note, most of the fabulous "Cache Cœur Naïf" EP is included, with Laetitia Sadier supplying her *voix sans vibrato* on some bright and breezy *chansons*. My only quibble: I would have taken out the relatively one-dimensional Konkret of "Rototon" and "7000" and put in instead the wonderful 'Lomo' dub version of "Bib" and the equally good 'Drykorn' mix of "Dark FX". But no matter, this CD is a priceless collection of totally original productions.

Autoditacker

Too Pure CD 1997

Niun Niggung

Sonig CD 1999

For the *Autoditacker* and *Niun Niggung* albums, Mouse on Mars made a decisive move away from the long, loose 4/4 workouts, like "Froschroom" and most of *Vulvaland*, and started to develop their songs into short, tightly-organised squiggles and squeaks of sound. These two albums represent some kind of apogee of their working practices up to the end of the 90s and they both achieved much more attention and recognition than they had thus far, with *Niun Niggung* even topping *The Wire* magazine's 50 Best Albums of 1999. In interview, St Werner and Toma have talked about their way of working in the studio during this period – deliberately pushing too much data through the channels, forcing the machines to improvise in order to deal with the overload. The moulded plastic surfaces of their music started to be put under stress and the music catches these disruptions and distresses. St Werner says, 'It's not exactly synchronised any more. This is rhythm – it's always beside the exact point, a bit behind it or a bit before it that makes a groove. Funk…'

On *Autoditacker*, "Tux & Damask" continued their flirtation with Jungle while "Juju" and "X-Flies" were whirling mobiles of sound hung in a playpen, filled with pin-sharp insect detail and flurries of digital interference. The intricacy of these arrangements continues on *Niun Niggung* on tracks such as "Distroia", an apocalyptic Jungle two-step workout, and was perhaps taken to its logical conclusion on "Super Sonig Fadeout". This heavily processed track, with its crunchy glitterbeats and vocoder, is a gloriously inventive effluence of junk-filled Garage, so stuffed with ideas that it can't possibly stay still, spilling out all over the shop. 'I really believe in the idea of experimental as *trying*; working towards new possibilities and newness,' St Werner says. "Super Sonig Fadeout" was another high water mark for Mouse on Mars and, if ever there was an obvious example needed for the playfulness in their music, this is it.

At the time of these two releases, Mouse on Mars were part of the so-called 'Neue deutsche Wellen' – a group of very talented artists/musicians, including Gas, Genf, Holosud, Pluramon and Wabi Sabi, all of whom lived and worked in and around Cologne and Düsseldorf. One of the centres of the scene was A-Musik, a shop and record label founded and run by Georg Odijk. Adjoining the shop was Odijk's flat, which he happened to share with St Werner and Markus Schmickler (Pluramon). These close social set-ups were reflected in their music and these two albums continued their long history of invitations to other sound and visual artists to contribute to their music and artwork. On *Autoditacker*, the magnificent Laika bassist, John Frennet, puts down a monster groove that fires and propels the motorik of "Tamagnocchi". On that same track (as well as many others on both albums), the live drumming is performed by Dodo Nkishi. French chanteuse and close friend Laetitia Sadier provided vocals for "Schnick Schnack Meltmade". To return Sadier's favour, St Werner and Toma played on and produced three tracks on Stereolab's 1997 LP *Dots and Loops*.

Idiology

Sonig CD 2001

Radical Connector

Sonig CD 2004

The abrasive 2-step lark of "Actionist Respoke", which opens *Idiology*, is bristling with clatterbox beats and hyperprocessed vocals and takes up exactly where *Niun Niggung* left off, as does the stuttering apokalypse-disko of second track, "Subsequent". Third track, "Presence", however, marks one of the siesmic shifts in the career of Mouse on Mars. Drummer Dodo Nkishi steps out from behind the drum kit and stands at the microphone, delivering a set of philosophically head-mashing lyrics about, er, presence. "The Illking" is another stark departure, this time into a pastoral coming together of synths, French horns and violins. There is the spirit of Copland and Ives' Americana running throughout, on "Catching Butterflies with Hands" and "Fantastic Analysis", a spirit started with *Niun Niggung*'s "Download Sofist". This all comes to a crunching halt with the 2-step oompah of "Doit" and gets a bit too much on "First : Break", a self-indulgent cacophony of directionless noise. But, overall, *Idiology* is another fine example of MoM's shapeshifting nature.

Radical Connector continues their zigzagging from style to style on each album, each more unpredictable and convoluted than the last. After the Baroque excesses of *Idiology*, *Radical Connector* is plush with hooks and beautiful pop melodies. The album sounds more like Basement Jaxx than Aphex Twin – an attempt to secure more mainstream commercial success? 'We thought it would be good to be more precise,' says Toma. The album's tracks are split down the middle, with half the lyrics being supplied again by Nkishi and the other half by close friend Niobe (aka Yvonne Cornelius), with her synthetically pristine vocals. Two of the Nkishi tracks open the album: "Mine Is in Yours" – a cacophony of chattering voices and a pileup of beats – and "Wipe that Sound", with its stomping funk bass and delirious falsetto whoops. For this listener, however, the more satisfying and intriguing songs are those sung by Niobe. The shudder and stutter of "The End", the sleek sheen of "Evoke an Object" are pure pop songs par excellence. Best of all is "Send Me Shivers", a very simple combo of mellow keys and crunchy beats and an outro heralded by strings, but a scintillating listening experience.

Live 04

Sonig CD 2005

doku/fiction

Kunsthalle Düsseldorf Book 2004

When 2004 came around, MoM celebrated their first 10 years with a live album and a book made up of commissioned artwork. As a duo, Mouse on Mars became very well-known for their very long and intense DJ sets of pounding Techno – "Twift Shoeblade" from *Autoditacker* and "Super Sonig Fadeout" from *Niun Niggung* were standout tracks that became live favourites. Since 1994, however, they also began touring as a band. London-based drummer Dodo Nkishi was drafted in to supplement their live performances, with Toma on bass and St Werner on keyboards. And what performances they were, too. I had heard that they were very good live but when I went to see them at the London Electric Ballroom in 1997, nothing prepared me for their full-on, surround-sound experience. Toma and Nkishi (wearing a T shirt that said I GOT THE CRABS) locked down the motorik dub grooves that night, nice and tight like Sly & Robbie, while St Werner unleashed a swirling cosmos of sounds from his very modest set-up of keyboards. The live album sticks to this band set-up and unsurprisingly features tracks from their most recent albums, except for the closing track, a monster version of the talismanic "Frosch".

How many bands publish a book to celebrate their 10th anniversary? Not many, but MoM did, but *doku/fiction* is more of an art gallery than a book proper. Once again calling on their outstanding contemporary artist and musician friends, MoM asked them to 'remix' Mouse on Mars in visual terms. What they got was paintings, photographs, pencil drawings, cut-ups, collages, cartoons, installations, scans, graphs and binary print-outs. My personal favourite is Adam Butler's "Piano score for a remix of the Mouse on Mars song "Twift" in the style of Eric [sic] Satie". The book also contains two very long and comprehensive interviews with Jan St Werner. When challenged by the interviewer that 'Not everyone can stomach what you dish up', St Werner's characteristically cryptic reply is: 'Granted. I couldn't say precisely who listens to it, apart from a group of musicians perhaps, but who might then probably say at some point, 7/8 would be great, but 7/8 has been done in Pop. It was prevalent in the 70s. King Crimson, Yes or Faust, CAN – there are loads of them, particularly in the genre of progressive rock and jazz.' But there is, after all, a musical element to the book. Included in the back is an exclusive CD collection of "9 Sound Models of 37 Imaginative Mappings", which comprises short pieces of pleasant but inessential electronica/Konkret, much better examples of which are "7000" and "Rototon" on their EPs, *Frosch* and *Bib*.

Yamo

Time Pie

EMI Electrola CD 1996

Von Südenfed

Tromatic Reflexxions

Domino CD 2007

Mouse on Mars have built their career on keeping their friends close, but they have also put themselves outside their comfort zone and collaborated with some singular (read 'challenging') figures in contemporary music. Recorded immediately after the *Glam* album, Yamo was the name for their collaboration with Kraftwerk's Wolfgang Flür. St Werner described their time with Flür recording *Time Pie*: 'He brought us to collapse. I think we all met at a level of what we call 'Schlager' [crass pop hits] in Germany. Not even Easy Listening, more like Easy Thinking.' It's true that the album contains some truly awful lyrics, but don't be put off – *Time Pie* is one of the unsung jewels in Mouse on Mars' crown and contains some genuinely gorgeous pop moments. The track "Aurora Borealis" has a deliciously icy sheen to it and an arctic stillness at its centre, all rooted in deep bass and dub spaciness. And, for some reason, I find the track "Naked Japanese" to be an astonishingly heavy four-and-a-half minutes, cresting and cresting to a climax before ebbing away on a wave of staccato synths.

For their collaboration with Mark E Smith, MoM renamed themselves Von Südenfed (yet another example of their jokey wordplay) and, as with Leftfield's collaboration with John Lydon, the resultant album proves to be surprisingly robust and solid. The record is awash with Smith's familiar barbed and droll lyrics, but the music is wildly different from the usual MoM fare. The obvious standout track is the insanely catchy, grimey, 2-steppy "Flooded", but most of the other tracks are pitched somewhere between rock and electro-clash. "The Young The Faceless And The Codes" is just squelchy bass synths and splattery drums, as is hit single "Fledermaus Can't Get It". "The Rhinohead" is pure Motown, "Dearest Friends" is Ladyship Black Mambazo playing Hawaii while "Chicken Yiamas" sounds like Blind Lemon Willy, for goodness' sake. The hilarious "Jbak Lois Lane" sees Mark E Smith arguing with a fella named Jack who is mowing his lawn. 'You know it's Sunday, don't you?' Smith asks. Singing in German for one song ("Speech Contamination / German Fear Of Österreich"), perhaps for Smith this collaboration was the nearest he could ever get to a collaboration with his beloved Can but, in lieu of that, this will do very nicely thank you. A versatile release with a smile on its face.

Varcharz

Ipecac Recordings CD 2006

Parastrophics

Monkeytown Records CD 2012

In interview, St Werner has revealed that *Varcharz* was made to break a publishing deal that he and Toma were unhappy with. It certainly is one of their weaker albums, in the sense that it lacks the same sense of fun as previous efforts. It also feels very unfocused. St Werner describes the album as 'odd and free. It's a mix of a rock and free jazz record.' And it shows. Most tracks are just crunchy beats and deconstructed bleepery and the worst of this tendency is evident in "Duul" and "Retphase", not enjoyable listens by any stretch of the imagination. It does, however, contain one classic killer MoM track, opener "Chartnok", which is another hugely inventive flirtation with Jungle rhythms.

After a six-year hiatus, Mouse on Mars reconvened for *Parastrophics*, one of their most coherent efforts for years. The album is awash with Prince-era synths and superbly-programmed stuttering, faltering beats. "Wienuss" is classic MoM – a highly-infectious, beautifully-controlled slice of white funk. The kick drum recalls Grandmaster Flash's "White Lines" and the track has the same HipHop forward movement. The barrage that is "Baku Hipster" has Space Invaders synths and a battering ram of bass drum. Startling. "They Know Your Name" has Dodo once again on vocal duty and carries on his contribution where *Radical Connector* left off, although this time round the track is far less abrasive and much more radio friendly. Closer "Seaqz" is a whiplash whiteout of mad synths, cracking snare and blips and bleeps of arcade games – pure electronic propulsion.

WOW

Monkeytown Records CD 2012

Spezmodia

Monkeytown Records CD 2014

21 Again

Monkeytown Records CD 2014

Parastrophics was an astonishing five years in the making and so, for their next release, MoM did the exact opposite – *WOW* was created from scratch in a matter of weeks, and released just six months after its predecessor. And you can feel this letting off of steam – *WOW* is a totally exuberant return to MoM's grass roots in the club scene with each track bouncing and bubbling along merrily. The track "ACD" even makes use of the much-loved Roland 303 and it's as if we were back in 1988. The vocal presence tying the whole mini-album together is Dao Anh Khanh, whom the band met during their tour of Asia 2011. Dao's shouty fantasy language recalls Damon Suzuki's similarly guttural pre-linguistic lyrics for CAN. The *Spezmodia* EP is an equally full-on fun fest. The club tracks here are all wonky Gabba/Happy Hardcore and tap into their days as a riotous duo live act, as evidenced on their tremendous 2014 appearance at the Boiler Room in Berlin. These excellent releases are MoM at their purest and simplest.

To mark a 20th anniversary, most bands would have put out a 'Best of' but, once again rejecting the conventional approach, MoM instead take one of the defining features of their career – collaboration – and use it on their anniversary release, *21 Again*. There are some very distinguished collaborators here, including friends old and new: Mark E Smith, Tortoise, Eric D Clarke, Laetitia Sadier, Schlammpeitziger, Junior Boys, FX Randomiz, Yoshimi from Boredoms, Matthew Herbert, composer Olivia Block and Oval. The release sees MoM up to their usual tricks of showing total irreverence for form and experimenting with content until it is bent completely out of shape: the ersatz disco of "Fertilised", faux rap of "Purple Frog", the quasi-soca of "Queen Für Erschein" (co-written with Dodo Nkishi) and the simulated Koncret with Oval on "Gitto Ski". "Key My Brain", "Putty Tart" and "Somiak" are the standout tracks and are already destined to become MoM classics. For the most part, this is a highly inventive addition to the MoM discography, bristling and brimming with ideas, but the quality threshold does occasionally drop. Somewhere in this double album a very good single CD is waiting to emerge.

MUSLIMGAUZE – A MANIFESTO

Muslimgauze is a musician named Bryn Jones, who died of septicaemia in 1999 at the age of 37.

Muslimgauze is the purest embodiment of the principles of dub that I've ever heard.

Muslimgauze produced the most delicate, shimmering, luminous dubs I've ever heard.

Muslimgauze produced the most brutal, ear-shredding industrial dubs I've ever heard.

Muslimgauze is Electro-raï, thick with percussion loops and live *zarb* routines processed through washing machine ambience.

Muslimgauze is HipHop, dreadnought dub and Industrial noise, Mego-style crackles, Technoid minimalism and Fourth World ambience.

Muslimgauze is voiceloops over heat 'n' dust instrumentals with raga drones and warping bass drums.

Muslimgauze is throbbing Arabic drumming, soft-edged dub bass, string drones and fragments of singing and guttural chanting in Arabic.

Muslimgauze is audio environments instead of songs; dub pressure – all bass energy and rhythmic complexity.

Muslimgauze's studio techniques include repetition, non-developmental processes, drones, drop outs and lots and lots of reverb.

Muslimgauze's signature in the studio is his use of the drop-out.

Muslimgauze's masterpiece may well be 'Drugsherpa', a delicate, shimmering, luminous 20-minute ghostly dub that uses found sound and processed field recordings of Middle-Eastern percussion.

Muslimgauze's music on 'Drugsherpa' is so layered and textured that it ceases to be
aural and exists almost solely in the realm of sight and touch.

Muslimgauze's 'Babylon Iz Iraq' remix for Unitone HiFi's track 'Babylon' is a dark unleashing of poltergeists and may well be his crowning achievement as a remixer.

Muslimgauze's world of music has four corners: Edgard Varèse, Kool Herc, Asian Dub Foundation & Throbbing Gristle (whom he saw live when he was 18).

Muslimgauze is Fourth World, Tribal hypnotica, Transcendental exotica.

Muslimgauze doesn't sound like anyone else; he was an originator.

Muslimgauze's productions is used by famed sound engineer Rashad Becker to sound check his PA and he says that Muslimgauze is the standard against which he measures other studio material.

Muslimgauze: "I was once in a Pakistani restaurant in Belgium and they were playing modern Pakistani music. I recognized Bryn's music in there. The way they cut their beats. When I came in, they turned it off and played traditional. And I said, 'No no, it's really good. Put on the original.' Bryn really liked this music, he really respected it and made his own version of it. You cannot chop up tradition that easily, but he was capable of doing that. His sounds give the impression it's loosely made, he distorts sounds, but it is someone in control to an extent that's very rare. It's like in martial arts, where someone's swinging a knife dangerously, but he knows to a millimetre what he is doing. It's just brilliant. He had this collage technique in one instance he had the reloading of a gun, and it was really well used; or giggling women, or crying women or the clapping of hands, it was edited so beautifully. All these layers have different stories. Through the whole CD you hear very deep stories; someone breathing, walking, and only if you listen carefully you hear that. These fine details, and like I said, the clapping of the hands and the loading, crying… strong images, simple, basic. You could also hear he'd been out listening to things. He said he was always in the studio, but that's not true. These musical styles he used, that's the sound of the time. He'd been tapping into things, but we don't know where, how or when. The dub, the breakbeat, all these elements he used he must have listened to. He wasn't disconnected, you could hear it." —Geert-Jan Hobijn, founder of Staalplaat.

"Muslimgauze was never sanitized. It was just full-on in-your-face, whether you liked it or not. Sometimes it was extremely uncomfortable, exacerbated by the fact that some titles had some very intense Middle Eastern things going on, it gave it that whole, very heavy underbelly – it was like a soundtrack to the hell of Gaza under Israeli occupation… But he wasn't making music for a Middle Eastern audience. To me it was the breaking of rules that was the beauty of it, because it was coming from somebody heavily influenced by the East. I was a guy who played by the rules, but Muslimgauze forced me to re-evaluate everything. He didn't play by any rules, he had his own thing going, that's what sets him apart from everybody else. You can see now, years after his death, how his influence is still out there. Muslimgauze lives on in other people. He lives on in my heart more than anything else." —John Bolloten, aka Rootsman.

Muslimgauze: "Even the slightest, prettiest tracks are inhabited (or inhibited) by an impossibly frail and inconceivably deep sadness – which, in truth, is hard to believe was entirely locatable in Jones's feelings about a Middle East he never visited and so which always remained an infinitely restorable phantasm inside his head. The sadness seems much deeper and further ingrained than that, approaching pathological – almost as if the terrible dispossessed 'birthright' of the Palestinians corresponded, secretly, to some personal scar or shadow in Jones's own life." —Ian Penman

Muslimgauze recalls the black arts, magic, murk and mental disintegration.

Muslimgauze is an assault on the senses.

Muslimgauze is an explosion in the cortex; a detonation in the solar plexus.

Muslimgauze is a shadow, an X-ray.

Muslimgauze is the negative of a track.

Muslimgauze is whatever you think he's not.

Muslimgauze is Punjab Root.

Muslimgauze is the Girl Who Sleeps with Persian Tulips.

Muslimgauze is the Fakir of Gwalior.

Muslimgauze is the Turkish Manipulator of Limbs.

Muslimgauze is Dharam Hinduja.

Muslimgauze is Feng Shui Orange.

Muslimgauze's music is boundless.

Muslimgauze is sounds of the *souk* and radio *muezzin*.

Muslimgauze is a call to arms.

Muslimgauze is the ghost in the machine.

Muslimgauze is the duppy in dub's machinery.

Muslimgauze is the turning of music inside out to show its seams.

Muslimgauze seeks out the concealed mechanisms.

Muslimgauze captures the sound of a machine's malfunction.

Muslimgauze is reshaped and remodelled.

Muslimgauze is lowered, louvred and heavily modified.

Muslimgauze is food.

Muslimgauze is primal.

Muslimgauze is maternal.

Muslimgauze began as Muslimgauze after Israel's invasion of the Lebanon in 1982.

Muslimgauze was born and lived his whole life in Swinton, Manchester and never set foot in the Middle East.

Muslimgauze's cover images and album / track titles are militant Arabic agit-prop.

Muslimgauze's political consciousness is extremely pro-Palestinian.

Muslimgauze: "There are no lyrics because that would be preaching."

Muslimgauze is often criticised for his political beliefs.

Muslimgauze always wore black socks with black sandals, black slacks and a dark hoody that made him look like a modern-day monk.

Muslimgauze's way of living bears a lot of similarities with the life of the French composer, Erik Satie, about whom I wrote a novel – both were one-offs, isolationist and totally committed to nothing other than their work.

Muslimgauze: "We work the whole time. It is like an illness."

Muslimgauze has, to date, released more than 200 albums, with still more being released every year.

Muslimgauze is, without doubt, the most gifted and prolific artist, arranger and producer in the world of electronica ever since John Cage made 'Imaginary Landscape No.1' in 1939 – a work for two variable-speed turntables, frequency recordings, muted piano and cymbal.

Muslimgauze's reputation as an innovator and pioneer is secure and his influence can be heard everywhere today, for instance in the dub bulletins of B-dum B-dum Sound, Saint Abdullah, Vatican Shadow, DJ Marcelle, Holy Tongue & Dark Sky Burial.

Muslimgauze is Janus, the god of beginnings, gates, transitions, time, duality, doorways, passages, frames and endings.

Muslimgauze is a shaman, a sorcerer.

Muslimgauze is a Romantic.

Muslimgauze is the Mozart of the post-techno era.

*Bryn Jones would have been 62 in 2023. There are 62 entries in this essay, one for each year of his life had he lived.

WALKING THE PENNINE WAY

IN 2020, after having completed 9 long distance walks around the UK, I decided I would try the mother of them all – the Pennine Way. At 268 miles, it's a serious mental and physical challenge. I have climbed Mt Blanc, which was also a serious mental and physical challenge, but I knew the PW would be just as challenging, albeit in different ways. In the summer of 2021, I started prepping for real. I joined a Facebook group dedicated to walking the PW and that summer I followed the journeys of several people as they completed the walk. It was a invaluable way to pick up tips on route finding, way-marking, weather, terrain, what-to-do's and what-not-to-do's. Through following those journeys, I built up a detailed picture of each stage – a kind of mood board – which was something I wouldn't realise was of such immense value until I actually started the walk myself. Then, in the month before I started, I did several long training walks of 2-3 days in the north of England, including the first stage of the PW itself. Everyone told me how tough the first two days on the PW were – many people give up at that point – so I did the first stage as a test-run to avoid any nasty surprises when I did it for real. The great day finally arrived on 8th June 2022 and I was all prepped and ready to start my 3-week trek. I was extremely glad to have already done that first stage as it gave me real confidence on the first day. The second day was also as tough as they say – the tortuous path up Laddow Rocks in particular was gruelling. But I did it. The third day involves a lot of flat walking by the sides of reservoirs and, feeling relieved at having done the first two days, I thought for the first time really that I could do it, that it was within my grasp.

But it was on the ninth day that the really great moment struck. I was walking a stage along the banks of the beautiful River Tees when the thought struck me that my mind and my body were in complete 'accordance' with the PW. It's a difficult feeling to describe, but I knew with clarity and certainty that I would be able to deal with whatever the PW threw at me. By this time, all blisters had healed and my body felt like a piece of well-oiled machinery that was functioning perfectly and working at its optimal level. But the meaning of the moment wasn't just about my physical fitness – anybody will get fit if they walk 15 miles a day for 9 days – it was mostly to do with my mind, which by that time had completely emptied itself of any thoughts whatsoever. Francis Bordeaux summed it up best when he said, 'In pilgrimage, we have an opportunity to de-centre ourselves. The pilgrim goes out to the other and returns as another person. It is a "detachment of the self", a self-emptying.' By that ninth day, my mind and body were not just in accordance with each other, they were in accordance with the landscape around me. I was not just passing through the landscape, I was the landscape itself. At that transcendent moment, I had a supreme sense of self-confidence and a profound sense of gratitude. This was my world and I had entered into and immersed myself in it fully. It was one of the most beautiful moments of my life.

STONE CROSS

'RICHARD, do something interesting with your life.'

There was admonishment in his voice when my old school friend Eddie said this to me. He was telling me off. A reprimand. Maybe even a warning. We were standing outside The Kings Head pub in Cuckfield, West Sussex, just after having said our goodbyes. He said this and then I watched him walk away. My first reaction was irritation. How dare he? Who did he think he was? What made him so perfect that he felt he could pass on advice to me? I walked away in the other direction, pissed off. Even now, it pisses me off a little bit.

I can't remember exactly when this happened. It was all so long ago. I think it was probably around 1987, which would make us both 22 years old. I remember it being summer? If it was summer 1987, then, in December of that year, I went on to study at International House, Piccadilly for the Preparatory Certificate in Teaching English as a Foreign Language (TEFL). I passed. In January 1988, I bought an inter-rail ticket and travelled to Milan to try to get a job teaching English. I remember I had to travel via Oostende – this was pre-Eurostar. Such was the demand for English by companies in and around Milan in the '80s that I ended up getting four jobs. I accepted one with Oxford Institutes Italiani, who had schools in Milan and Magenta, and stayed in Italy for the next two years. But that's another story.

Did Eddie know this when I met him at The Kings Arms? If he did, his reprimand was even meaner. Wasn't travelling to a new country, whose language I didn't know, and living there for two years, an interesting thing to do? I'd have thought so. Why didn't he?

Or, more realistically, he probably didn't know. If I knew when I met him at The Kings Head that I was going to study for a TEFL certificate, I can't believe that I wouldn't have told him, so maybe I hadn't yet applied. Or even known about the course. Maybe his parting shot inspired me to search for something interesting to do and, when I found out about the TEFL course, apply for it. Who knows. In any case, it turned out that this would be the last time I ever saw Eddie.

In 1978, I started my third year at Oathall Secondary School in Haywards Heath, West Sussex. I was 13. My class was called 3J1. In the first year, it was 1J1, in the second 2J1, and now 3J1. We were the same group of kids throughout and we were about to start our third year together. We were a tight unit. I remember the names of some of the other kids – Huw Brown, Peter Boyer, Stephen Dewhurst, Ian Pickering (Pickers?), Susan Paternoster (yes, really), Lindsay Whatshername, Judith Thingimijig. It all gets a bit hazy after that. I remember their faces and nicknames better. There was Tuppence (because he was so small), Bogey, Foggy, Chalky. Many years later, I remember wondering how on earth I had got away with five years at school without anyone cottoning on to the fact that they could have called me Dick Skinner.

But, in September 1978, there was a new kid in class, whose name was Eddie Stone. He had joined us from a local prep school called Great Walstead. I'm sure it's exactly the same now as it was then in small provincial towns that have both state and private schools, but there was a great deal of animosity between us and the posh boys. And Eddie was posh. His family lived in a beautiful 17th century house, called Upper Lodge, in Ardingly, a quiet (and very expensive) village just outside Haywards Heath. I seem to remember his father worked in the City. On his first day at Oathall, Eddie carried a leather satchel and wore grey flannel shorts. Shorts! He had the mickey taken out of him about that for years afterwards. He never lived it down.

For some reason, Eddie was told to sit next to me in registration. For the rest of Secondary school – three years – we sat next to each other in registration from 9-9.25am five days a week. We also sat next to each other in English, Geography and a lot of other classes. I like to think that, because I was probably the first person he got to know when he arrived at Oathall, he naturally gravitated towards me. Wishful thinking. But I do remember hours and hours spent at our pair of desks, listening to white-haired Mr Poulson in his three-piece suit in English classes reading from Arthur Conan Doyle's *The Lost World*, Eddie on the right hand side facing forward and me on the left, so that, when we were writing, because Eddie was left handed, we would be facing each other. I can picture Eddie's handwriting clear as day, even now. We used the same kind of Parker pen.

But the thing that connected us most strongly was our mutual love of the Lake District. In the summer before I started secondary school, my dad and I climbed Yr Wyddfa (Snowdon). This was the summer of 1976, the hottest summer on record for years. There was a drought on and water bans were in place everywhere. We took the route via Crib Goch, an arête whose name in Welsh means 'red ridge'. It's not for the faint hearted, but I was a fearless 11-year-old.

When we got back down, we went for a swim in a lake because the showers at Pen-y-Pass youth hostel where we were staying were banned. Just as I was about to dive under the water, I felt a sudden rushing, as though a tap had been turned on in my body. It turned out that I had stepped on a broken bottle, which made deep cuts in my big toe and ball of my foot. With no hospitals anywhere nearby, we were told about a convent up in the mountains which had a treatment centre, so my dad drove me there. The nuns told me to stand in a bowl of hot water, which I knew would open up the wound again. I said I didn't want to, but the nuns told me I had to because they needed to check for broken glass inside my foot. I was terrified, but I did so and the bowl soon turned red with blood. With the all clear, they put butterfly stitches on the cuts, which afterwards felt like the buzzing of a dodgy electrical connection. We drove back home the next day and I have never returned to north Wales since. It felt cursed.

The following year, my dad and I switched our attention to the Lake District. I planned all the routes, wrote the letters to all the youth hostels to book beds, dad signed the cheques. We then spent every one of my school holidays climbing as many of the 214 fells as possible, eventually bagging the last few in the summer of 1981 after my final year at school. On the last climb, we carried a bottle of fizz up and opened it on the summit.

When Eddie arrived at Oathall, I found out that he shared my obsession with all things to do with mountaineering. He had been visiting the Lakes for years with his family, too. When I sat my Geography O level, Eddie and I just happened once again to be sitting next to each other. I opened the paper and saw that one of the questions was all about the geology and agriculture of the Lake District. I looked up at Eddie and we smiled at each other. We both got As. This was the thing that bonded us. For us, mountains were theatres for dreams.

By the end of school, there was a group of us that hung out together: me, Eddie, Steven B, Mark S, Mark T and Neil A. In the summer holidays after school finished, we went on a camping trip in the Ashdown Forest. We had terrible tents and too little food. It was hot.

Arguments broke out and we cut short the trip and went home. The next month, we all went on to the local sixth-form college together. On the first morning of sixth form, I went to my registration group and who should be there? Eddie. Once again, we sat next to each other every day for the next two years.

By now, Eddie was a dedicated follower of fashion. At college, he wore Kickers, a mustard-coloured pair of dungarees and Fruit of the Loom sweatshirts. He smoked weed, listened to Bob Marley and the Tom Robinson Band and wore a feather earring in his left ear. He had come a long way from his satchel and shorts. He was cool. Cooler than anyone else. Way cooler than me.

Throughout college, Eddie and I went out with many of the same girls. My first girlfriend was Nicky W, whom I unceremoniously dumped one night at a party. I had no good reason and I'll never forget the look of hurt on her face when I told her. I regret that. She ended up going out with Eddie. Along the way, we also both went out with Helen M and Jess S.

And then there was Kim, who loved Fleetwood Mac and Bob Dylan and dressed like a Rolling Stones groupie. I had never met a girl like her before. I didn't know how to handle her. She blew hot and cold and was hard to read. She had a sharp tongue and wasn't afraid to use it. It was years later that I understood all this was just a form of self-defence. She got kicked out of college after only a month due to lack of attendance. The nerve of her.

She, Eddie and I had a *Jules et Jim* type relationship for a short time but it never really happened between me and Kim. We never got it together. She and Eddie, however, were a perfect match and they had an on-off thing over the next few years. I knew on some level I was jealous. Despite that, Kim and I managed somehow to maintain a friendship, which has lasted to this day, although we haven't seen each other in a long time.

After college, I drifted. I had failed my A levels badly and didn't know what to do. I got some casual work in the industrial estate in Haywards Heath. Some of my friends were drifting too. On days off, Steven and I would meet in pubs at lunchtime, play Juno First all afternoon and get drunk. At the local social club, Steven, Neil and I played snooker against people older than us that we used to be afraid of at school. Eddie was no longer around at this time. He had moved to north Wales to become an outward bound instructor. I was impressed. While the rest of us were stumbling around, Eddie seemed to have found the way forward for himself.

I knew I had to get out of Haywards Heath as well. If I stayed any longer, I would never leave, and I didn't want anything that Haywards Heath had to offer. Out of sheer desperation, one day Mark S and I decided to move to London. It was April 1985. A room had come up in my sister's friend's house, which Mark and I shared. I signed up with a temping agency doing soul-destroying jobs and Mark worked long hours as a waiter. Anything to pay the rent.

I have a photograph I took of Eddie sitting opposite me on a London tube train and giving me the V sign. It was definitely taken on the London Underground so it must have been taken after I moved to London. I have no idea why we were together in London or where we were going. No memory at all. Our paths had diverged. He had pursued the path that we had both started as young teenagers in the Lakes, which Eddie had then explored more fully throughout our college years by taking up rock climbing seriously, whereas I had pulled away, moved to London, met a girl and continued to drift for the next year or two.

Then that meeting at The Kings Head in 1987 and his comment that made me bristle so. I seem to remember that, by then, not only was Eddie happily working as an outward bound instructor in north Wales, but was also sharing a cottage with his girlfriend. It sounded idyllic. I still hadn't done anything with my life, yet his seemed to be all sorted out. Maybe my irritation was about my dissatisfaction with myself rather than with Eddie's words. Yes, that's it. His comment had touched a nerve. Maybe he knew me better than I realised. Maybe his comment was an encouragement, not a criticism. I had almost certainly misjudged him.

The next few years for me were TEFL teaching in Italy for two years, then back to England to study for an English Literature degree at Sussex University, something I had decided to try for while in Italy. At 24, I had got in as a mature student rather than on my terrible science A level grades. Looking back, it was a huge moment in my life. It was the first time that I'd felt a sense of direction and purpose. I savoured every moment of my degree. I didn't know what the outcome would be, but I knew I was finally on the right path.

A few months after I finished studying at Sussex, I went back to Haywards Heath to visit my dad and step mum for the weekend. In the kitchen, drinking tea, my step mum told me that Eddie had died in a climbing accident.

What?

The details were sketchy, she said. Apparently, Eddie had gone free climbing solo, without telling anyone, including his girlfriend, where he was going or when he would be back. All this was highly unusual for any experienced climber, but especially for someone who had been trained as an outward bound instructor. I recall understanding that, because of all this, it was many days before anyone found his body.

Why hadn't he used ropes? Why go out alone? Obviously he had put himself in such a position that if he made any kind of mistake, even a tiny one, the consequences would be fatal. Why? Knowing Eddie as I thought I did, I just didn't understand what had driven him to put himself in such a precarious, dangerous place.

I wrote a letter of condolence to his parents but never received a reply. Then I heard a rumour that the whole family had moved away suddenly. Weirdly, I remember his older sister Emma and his younger sister Charlotte really well. The grief was too unbearable, I presumed. I don't think I felt grief, exactly. I was shocked and confused. So young. Why? Was he unhappy? Did he go out knowing he wouldn't come back? All the signs were there – leaving secretly without telling anyone, climbing solo with no rope. Madness. Or not? Did he want to die? Eddie was always streets ahead of me in terms of being more certain about life choices. Was he ahead of me in this, too?

All I had were questions that would never be answered. No one was there at the moment of death to record the exact circumstances. Eddie's death has haunted me all my life but I've had to learn how to accept that there will never be any answers. All that remains of him are a few snaps that have changed colour like autumn leaves, some shaky memories and that awful final image in my mind's eye of him losing contact with the rock face, arms flailing, legs bicycling, floating through air.

On 21st August 2024, an acquaintance of mine messaged me to tell me that a close mutual friend of ours, Adrian, had died in a climbing accident in Wales.

Fuck!

I can't believe it. This can't be happening. Ade was a fully fit and healthy man. How on earth could he have died? My acquaintance didn't know anything, only that he had fallen. Over the next 48 hours, I remained in a state of shock. It was so surprising that I would never see him again. Slowly, details emerged. It turned out that Ade was climbing Yr Wyddfa and that he was alone. Later, I found out that he was actually on Crib Goch when he fell. Two other climbers saw him fall and it was them who called the Mountain Rescue Team. Apparently, it took the MRT two hours to get there but I still didn't know if they found Ade dead or alive.

The nearest MRT is in Llanberis. From there, it is a five-mile drive to the car park at Pen-y-Pass. Crib Goch is at 923m. The average time it takes to climb Yr Wyddfa from Pen-y-Pass via Crib Goch is four hours. The time it took for the Llanberis MRT to muster, drive to Pen-y-Pass and then get to where Ade was on Crib Goch was just two hours, which is an absolutely superhuman effort. It struck me that the only way the two other climbers could have known that it only took them two hours to get to Ade was if they had stayed with him. That they stayed with Ade gave me some comfort but I was still desperate to know what happened.

I first met Ade (whose surname is Cross) in 2007, when he enrolled onto the Creative & Life Writing MA at Goldsmiths University, London, where I was a tutor. Since finishing university in 1992, I had gone on to complete a Masters in Creative Writing and then managed to publish a novel. On the back of that, in 2002, I landed a job teaching at Goldsmiths. I was assigned as Adrian's one-to-one mentor.

The first thing I noticed about Ade was that he and his writing were very funny. And scatty. He wrote hilarious and surreal stories about things like trying to catch rattlesnakes in parks. We became fast friends and I gradually learned more about him. He had studied Philosophy at Lancaster University and was now working as an Education Officer for refugees for Wandsworth Council. Wow, I thought, that's a worthy job. I quickly realised that Ade was a highly-principled man with solid socialist leanings and a strong sense of social justice. He had spent the summer of 2016 in Palestine helping to rebuild housing that had been destroyed. How many other people did I know who would do that? Not many. No one, actually, including me.

In 2011, I started a live monthly reading series called Vanguard Readings. Ade was its number one fan. He would come along to every event without fail. He was so reliable and trustworthy that I asked him to host some of the events. He stepped up to the mark with relish and his introductions to the readers became legendary for their dry wit and eccentricity.

In 2014, I formed a publishing branch of the reading series, called Vanguard Editions. Our first publication was an anthology of short stories. I asked Ade and a friend of ours, Des, to be the editors. They both enthusiastically agreed and did a great job. Ade and Des, along with another Goldsmiths graduate, Kat, became Vanguard's Trustees.

In 2013, myself, Ade, my climbing partner Sam, my wife and my wife's friend went on a walking trip to the Lake District. We stayed near Bowness and climbed Loughrigg and Bowfell. I'd never seen Ade happier. But this was peanuts for him. He used his holiday time to go on very active, sometimes extreme trips. He went whitewater rafting in the croc-infested Zambezi, on a long sledding trip north of the Arctic Circle in the depths of winter. He would travel alone to the Cairngorms and traipse around them with nothing but a bivouac. No tent. No phone signal. This last trip alarmed me. I've been walking in the Highlands and I know how wild they are. One foot in a rabbit hole and you're screwed. I urged him not to go out solo like that again without some way of being in contact.

Over the years, I saw Ade very regularly at the Vanguard Trustee meetings as well as readings, launches and other events. The last time I saw him was in April 2024 when he agreed to sit with me all day at the Poetry Fair in London, where Vanguard had a stall of books to sell. I asked him for his help and he gave up his whole Saturday, without question, to support a press he wholeheartedly believed in. That was the measure of the man.

In the weeks that followed Ade's death, I waited for more news. I decided I would attend his inquest. I kept an eye on the website for the Coroner's Office in Gwynedd, but nothing came up for months. Ade's funeral was in September but, I was away and couldn't go. I was really gutted that I couldn't get to say my farewells. To my dismay, I was out of the country when his inquest was finally announced. Des, however, was able to attend and he passed on to me some details that were outlined at the inquest.

Apparently, Ade had arrived at the B&B in Betws-y-Coed where he was staying at around 7pm on Friday 16th August. The following morning, he exchanged pleasantries with the other guests, commenting on what a lovely day it was, such good weather for walking. He seemed happy. He left at around 8am.

He was seen falling from the heights of Crib Goch by another walker at about 11am. The rescue services were called. They found him with severe injuries consistent with a tumbling fall from height. He was pronounced dead at the scene. Close by his body were his notebook and a novel, *Drive Your Plough over the Bones of the Dead*, by Olga Tokarczuk. In his pocket were some fridge magnets, which said 'I climbed Snowdon'. The coroner said his boots had a good tread and were suitable for the terrain.

I winced at the title of that book. It was so typical of Ade that he would be carrying a hefty novel with him up a mountain; not only that, but a hefty Polish novel in translation by a Nobel-prize-winning author. He was a ferocious reader. But that title. Then there was Crib Goch, the red ridge. I googled pictures of it and couldn't believe how perilous it looked. I couldn't believe I'd climbed it aged 11. Perhaps that's the best age to do it, when you have no inkling of the danger. Did Ade have that inkling? Any fear? I doubt it. He was a maverick, never one to turn down a challenge.

So, it was a solo walker who spotted him, not a pair. And the words 'a tumbling fall from height' suggests the fall was sheer and that Ade had died quickly, but who knows? No one, and no one ever will. I just hope he died quickly, with little or no pain.

Those magnets raise a question. All common sense would say that he must have bought them at the shop on the summit, which suggests that he was on his way down when he fell. But Ade fell at 11am. I'm assuming Ade caught a bus, or took a taxi, from Betws-y-Coed to the car park at Pen-y-Pass. That journey would have taken about 20 minutes. From there, the average time to the summit of Yr Wyddfa is four hours. So if Ade had caught the bus, climbed to the summit, bought the magnets and then was on his way down, all in just three hours, he must have been moving very fast. My feeling is that he was on his way up. If so, the fact that he took three hours to get to Crib Goch would fit in with the average four-hour journey time to the summit. If that is the case, where did he get the magnets? I'll never be sure.

So that was the end of the road for me. Ade had died in a tragic mountaineering accident. Just like that. I was left with a mountain of good memories of a kind man, funny and original, clumsy and loveable. Gone too young. The same age as me. His boots with a 'good tread' making one wrong move amongst the rocks on the red ridge, then a terrible chute through air, floating.

The news about Ade immediately triggered memories of Eddie and, for those first few days after Ade's shocking death, I was also transported back in time to Eddie's death 32 years earlier. While I waited for further news about Ade, I started to ransack my memories about Eddie and his death. All I knew was that he went free climbing solo without telling anyone and that it was a few days before his body was found. I needed to find out more.

On Facebook, I reconnected with Mark T and Steven B. I asked if they had any information about Eddie's death but they only knew as much as I did. I asked Kim for her memories and stories about Eddie and she sent me photos of us all at college and told me what she remembered. We talked about Eddie a great deal but, she said, she had 'virtually no memory' of him. I understood. For me, too, it was hard to picture what I did with Eddie. We spent so much time together between the ages of 13 and 19 but I can remember precious little about him.

The fact that he was alone, used no ropes and told no one where he was going always perturbed me. Had he gone out that day knowing he would not come back? When I tentatively put that to Kim, she was adamant that there was no question of suicide. 'No never!! Hubris might have killed him but in a million years he would never have taken his own life,' she said. But Kim went on to say that Eddie had once said to her that he knew he would die young. He died at 27 years old, the same age as Jimi, Janis, Jim, Kurt and Amy. Eddie always had the whiff of a rock star about him.

I googled endlessly about climbers in north Wales but came

up blank. Eddie died in 1992, just pre-internet, so there was next to nothing about him online. And then I found a quote by a climber, who said, 'I watched Ed Stone down climb Axle Attack taking his gear out on the way.' That was tantalising. It sounded as though the climber was impressed. Then I found another reference to Eddie by another climber, who just said that he remembered 'going back many times to Wales to stay with and climb with the late Ed Stone.' To hear Eddie being called Ed by these people was strange for me. I realised that these guys probably knew Eddie better than I did. They had a new name for him. Eddie was reborn as Ed in north Wales. He'd found his true place and calling.

I wrote to the Coroner's Office in Gwynedd asking for a Record of Inquest for Eddie. The only information I could give them was his name, that he died somewhere in north Wales and the year of his death. They couldn't find anything with so little to go on. I was at a dead end.

Then Kim sent some more photos. She had been digging a bit deeper and had found a photo of Eddie roped up on a rock face in mid-climb. He's wearing grey lycra pants and a peach-coloured T shirt. It was terribly moving to see him in action like this. So young. Kim had also found the original clipping from the local paper, the Mid Sussex Times, about Eddie's death. This turned out to be the crucial turning point in my effort to discover the facts. It said:

> A FORMER Mid Sussex man has been killed in a climbing accident in Wales.
>
> Psychology student Edward Stone, 27, died in a fall on Snowdon while climbing solo.
>
> Mr Stone, son of Judith and Reg Stone, who used to live in Upper Lodge, Ardingly, was a mature student at Bangor University. He had lived in Wales for some years.
>
> A keen and experienced climber, he had set out on the expedition fully equipped on Friday. Royal Air Force rescue crews and the Llanberis Mountain Rescue team discovered his body the following day. The cause of the accident is unknown.

The funeral will be held today (Friday) at Llanberis parish church.

The first detail that leapt out at me was that he had died on Yr Wyddfa, as Ade had. No way. Then I noticed the words 'fully equipped'. So he wasn't free climbing. Also, the fact that he was found the following day meant that someone raised the alarm quickly after Eddie failed to return home that night. Finally, that the Llanberis MRT found him so quickly suggests they knew where to look, which in turn suggests that whoever raised the alarm knew where Eddie had gone. All this refutes any idea that Eddie had acted recklessly that day to ensure he wouldn't return, which is a source of great comfort.

The clipping showed me that I had believed a false story about Eddie's death all these years. He wasn't free climbing at all, so why had I believed he was? Who told me? How did I pick that up? And it wasn't days before his body was found – it was found pretty fast, actually. Far from being a solitary, lonely, possibly suicidal event, it was instead a tragic, unexpected accident and the alarm was raised very quickly by someone close to him.

Kim had added the date by hand to the clipping – October 1992. With this less vague date, plus the names of Eddie's parents and other information, I wrote once again to the Coroner's Office. This time, after a week or two, I received the Record of Inquest for Eddie, which provided even more clues. It said his injuries were:

    1a) Acute cardio-respiratory failure due to
    1b) Fracture dislocation of the neck due to
    1c) Consistent with a fall from a height
    2 Diffuse subarachnoid haemorrhage and fracture of skull

A quick google revealed that a 'subarachnoid haemorrhage' was usually the result of a blow to the head and a 'fracture dislocation of the neck' was usually the result of a fall from a significant height. This information, plus the fractured skull, suggests that Eddie, when he fell, landed on his head.

The Record also said that Eddie's body was found at the base of Trinity Gully. I researched this online and found images of Trinity Face – an enormous, sheer rock face hanging just below the summit of Yr Wyddfa that looked like a miniature version of the north face of the Eiger. There are four routes up Trinity Face: Great Gully, Little Gully, Left-hand Trinity and Central Trinity. 'Trinity Gully' didn't tell me which route exactly Eddie was on at the time of his death but all four, more-or-less vertical, ascents looked terrifying.

But what I still struggled with was why the ropes hadn't saved him when he lost contact with the rock. I presume he had hooked himself onto crabs at pretty tight, regular intervals so that, if he did fall, he wouldn't have fallen far or harmed himself. But the injuries Eddie sustained suggest a fall from a great height, which doesn't tally with that idea. Once again, I will never have an answer to this question. No one was there to witness the fall. Eddie's secret will remain with him forever.

Eddie's death is a distant memory for me, and an unreliable one, it turns out. I had misremembered him, and therefore misrepresented him, for years. I can't say with certainty that I knew Eddie well. Did I ever? Those teenage years are tumultuous. You go through so many changes – layers, even – so quickly, make bad decisions, mistreat people. Ade's death is brand new in relative terms, more raw, but I knew what kind of person Ade was from the off. Soulful, good-natured. They were different characters from different moments in my life but, because they were both friends who died on the same mountain, they will be forever tethered in my mind. But what was the tether? A leyline? A tightrope? Ariadne's thread? Their deaths were caused by tiny errors, a boot put in slightly the wrong place, a fingertip in a fingerhold not exerting quite enough pressure. Narrow margins. I had also passed over that terrain and mercifully had escaped with nothing but cuts in the foot. I was lucky.

I want to end this piece with something I discovered during those many days researching Eddie's death. I found out that, following Eddie's death, a climber friend of his (or friends, I don't know) put up and named a new route after him. The route is an E7 Trad climb on a mountain called Gallt yr Ogof, which is approximately seven miles north east of Yr Wyddfa. The route is called *Heart of Stone*. Far from being forgotten, Eddie will always be remembered by those who knew him best.

INTERVIEW WITH THE WOMBWELL RAINBOW

WR: When and why did you start writing poetry?

RS: I remember writing my first poem when I was 15 and still at school. It was about the First World War, biplanes and castles – a real adventure. It was so exciting. I carried on writing bad love poetry to girlfriends throughout my teens. Then I joined the poetry society at uni. I've been writing poetry all my life and I'm sure I will end my life in a bath chair trying to write a poem.

Who introduced you to poetry?

I remember reading T.S. Eliot's poems about cats aloud in class when I was 12 or so. Macavity the mystery cat made a big impression on me. The next big thing was discovering a beautiful book of words and images about the Lake District called *Presences of Nature*, which included poems by Roy Fisher, Roger Garfitt, Frances Horovitz and Norman Nicholson as well as incredible black and white photographs of the fells and lakes by John A. Davies, Fay Godwin and Paul Joyce. I was 17 at the time. A couple of years later, I came across Ted Hughes' collection *Remains of Elmet* published in a book accompanied by stunning black & white photos of the Pennines by Fay Godwin. I would say that these two books were the start of everything for me. The pairing of the visual with words was revelatory and instilled in me a lifelong love of the sense of place in poetry.

How aware are and were you of the dominating presence of older poets traditional and contemporary?

I was mostly aware of the Romantics when I started reading and writing poetry but Wordsworth and the others leave me cold, I'm afraid. The Victorians (Tennyson, etc), too. Later, I discovered the Metaphysical poets, whom I love. And I love "Gawain & the Green Knight". My interest as a poet really starts with the First World War poets. Wilfred Owen's poetry is amazing. That led to Keith Douglas, whose work is also amazing. And then everything that followed. And, of course, whichever way I look, there is always T.S. Eliot.

What is your daily writing routine?

No daily routine. I write whenever the urge luckily comes, wherever I happen to be. For me, travelling is a good time to write.

What subjects motivate you to write?

Everything around me and inside me. Playfulness. Lyricism. Nature. Culture.

What is your work ethic?

No ethic as such.

How do the writers you read when you were young influence your work today?

I think those poems that I read early on have left a lasting impression on me. I have always found Wallace Stevens' work fascinating – his poem "Tea at the Palaz of Hoon" is a favourite of mine – and I would say that I have favourite poems rather than poets. When I was living in Italy, I used the British Council library a lot and came across a wonderful short poem there by Lotte Kramer called "White Morning", which left an indelible impression on me. Yeats' "The Wild Swans at Coole" made a similarly big impression, as did Geoffrey Hill's "A Song from Armenia" and Anne Stevenson's "Utah". Some of Donald Davie's early poems I like a lot, including his "Ezra Pound in Pisa". That leads me on to Pound, whose Imagist Manifesto is still meaningful to me. Wallace Stevens' "Thirteen Ways of Looking at a Blackbird" is the very embodiment of Imagism and a wonderfully alive poem. Stevens' poem "The Dwarf" is one of the weirdest and most wonderful poems I've ever read. Stevens' poem "The Snow Man". Sylvia Plath, Ian Hamilton, Paul Muldoon, Keith Douglas. I read all these poems/poets when I was in my teens/20s and they have stayed with me forever.

Whom of today's writers do you admire the most and why?

The titans David Harsent, Paul Muldoon, Peter Didsbury, then Mona Arshi, Catherine Ayres, Clodagh Beresford Dunne, Jane Burn, Chaucer Cameron, Marion Christie, Josephine Corcoran, Anthony Costello, Emma Danes, Nichola Deane, Steve Ely, Cathy Galvin, Peter Gizzi, Lavinia Greenlaw, Jeff Hilson, Lisa Kelly, Zaffar Kunial, Sylvia Legris, Roy Marshall, Richie McCaffery, Nicola Nathan, Eiléan Ní Chuilleanáin, Alice Oswald, Anita Pati, Deborah Randall, Pete Raynard, Denise Saul, Zoë Skoulding, Pauline Stainer, Julian Stannard, Paul Stephenson, Michael Symmons Roberts, Marion Tracy,

Julian Turner, Kate Wakeling, Sarah Westcott, Judith Willson, Samantha Wynne-Rhydderch.

Why do you write, as opposed to doing anything else?

No choice, I'm afraid. Poems, for me, are traces of my existence.

What would you say to someone who asked you 'How do you become a writer?'

Read widely and deeply.

Tell me about the writing projects you have on at the moment.

My next project is a small collection of fractal poems, a kind of poetry I've only recently discovered.

How did you decide on the order of the poems in your book?

In the case of *White Noise Machine*, I placed the four "Songs", which are cut-ups of lines taken from spiritual pop songs, every quarter of the way through the collection. They act as the four cornerstones of the collection really and they 'house' all the other poems. Once I'd done that, I made sure that the several little 'runs' of three or four poems were evenly spaced throughout. Then there were lots of obvious pairings that I made sure were on facing pages: the chicory and lavender poems, the two playful poems based on Irish poets, "Lix" and "Aran", which are both places in Scotland and the two pantoums "Hub" and "Hem".

Noting the various locations in your book how important is the 'sense of place' in it?

Oh, crucial, I'd say! A great deal of my work is about being/walking in a landscape. In *White Noise Machine*, there are several poems written *in situ* or *en route*. My wife and I went on retreat for the month of December in 2022 to Mevagissey in Cornwall, which was a cosmic experience. The "Three Cornish Landscapes" were written there, written as I was watching the sunrise happen and the days pass. Those three poems are attempts to recreate that sense for the reader of the wonder of those places that I originally felt. "The Scene" was also written in Cornwall, in response to the breathtaking sea- and skyscapes down there. I like to think of them as Impressionist paintings with a dash of the energy of Abstract Expressionism thrown in. The three poems collected together as "A Northern Archive", on the other hand, were all written while I was walking the Pennine Way last summer. A passed a copse of fir trees and wrote the poem in my head as I walked. The same with "Lapwing", birds whose cries pierced me nearly every day on the way. "Accordance" was my attempt at describing the way in which you can fuse with the landscape as you walk in it and it took several days to get it right. "Lix", too, was written while doing a long distance walk, this time the Rob Roy Way in Scotland last September. Near the route, there is a place called Lix, apparently so called because it used to be a Roman encampment. As I was walking from Killin to Kenmore along the shore of Loch Tay, I was wondering what it must have been like for the local people when the Romans were there. I wrote the poem in my head and, when I arrived in Kenmore, I wrote it down as is. These places – Cornwall, the Pennines, Scotland – are all inspirational to me. They breathe the poems into me and I exhale them.

How intentional is describing your work in terms of other creative pursuits such as painting (Impressionists) and music (*White Noise Machine*)?

Um, well, "Three Cornish Landscapes" are obviously meant to be very visual poems, but I mentioned Abstract Expressionism because I didn't want the poems to be entirely descriptive; there is supposed to be an energy in them that transcends the purely visual. There is immense energy in the Cornish sea and sky and I wanted to convey that. As far as the musical is concerned, music runs through the poems in this collection like the current in the river. Throughout the poems I've woven in the voices/mimes of David Bowie, Kate Bush, Luc Ferrari, Flaming Lips, Peter Gabriel, Genesis, Christopher Hobbs, Joni Mitchell, Muslimgauze, Éliane Radigue & R.E.M.. The four Songs that I mentioned earlier are cut-ups and are composed of lines cut from spiritual pop songs. These cut-ups have been an ongoing project since lockdown and began with a cut-up of the Talking Heads song, "Once in a Lifetime". That cut-up, titled "Life in a Oncetime", was the closing poem of my book *Dream into Play*, which came out last year. I put out a whole book of cut-ups of pop songs with Vanguard Editions in January this year. The Songs in *White Noise Machine* were composed in a very particular way: I tried to find two spiritual pop songs that shared a common theme, then cut lines from them into couplets. The couplets were then ordered and repeated via a highly organised pattern. The repetition is supposed to be incantatory and I wanted the poems to act as a balm, a salve for the soul. The whole cut-up process is absolutely alchemical and magical. As William Burroughs said, "When you cut into the present, the future leaks out."

Why is the cut up method "alchemical and magical" to you?

The very first cut-up I did was actually a cut-up of two songs by R.E.M. – "Finest Worksong" and "Ignoreland", called "Finest Ignoreland" – which I posted online just before the American election in January 2021. It was a plea to Americans to do the right thing and vote Biden in. It worked! I chose those two songs of theirs because they shared a very similar political theme – insurrection, protest, etc. – so that one was relatively straightforward to do. I then made the Talking Heads cut-up. I then broadened the remit and looked at making cut-ups, not from a single song or two songs by the same band, but two songs from different bands as well. The first one I did like that was a cut-up of Nick Drake's "Northern Sky" and Fleetwood Mac's "Landslide" called "Northern Landslide". When I thought about those two songs, I realised they subtly shared a theme, i.e. a landscape that expressed a state of mind. They are both songs about doubt, about expressing vulnerability. Sometimes, the songs I chose shared a much more obvious theme – like the references to drug use in Prince's "Sign o' the Times" and "White Lines" by Melle Mell. Sometimes it was about genre. I've always loved Blue Öyster Cult's "(Don't Fear) the Reaper" but what to cut it with? I'm not a huge Heavy Metal fan and know nothing about Metallica other than their most famous song is "Enter the Sandman", so I looked at that and, lo and behold, they were both gothicky fairytales. Sometimes, it was the song titles that drew me – I couldn't resist making a cut-up of Blur's "Tender" with Heaven 17's "Temptation", for example. The only reason I cut "Manic Monday" with "Ruby Tuesday" is because of the days of the week in the titles. Those songs have nothing in common so it was more of a challenge, but it works – the poem is common ground between the two but unlike either song. It is its own thing. That's what's alchemical and magical about the process – you are taking two things and cutting them together to create a third thing, something new, something that didn't exist before, that has its own voice and meaning.

What cut up process do you use once you have found the material? Is it a conscious process, or arbitrary?

Very conscious. I blow up and print out the lyrics, literally cut them up with scissors and then scatter them on the living room floor. Then I cast my eyes over them, trying to find lines that will go well together, to create a flow. There is meaning there somewhere but you have to find it. It's a bit like dowsing. Although this process is quite conscious, the form of the resultant poem is arbitrary. I never go in thinking that this poem has to be 14 lines long, or has to have four stanzas, or whatever. The material dictates the form. One of the best cut-ups I've ever done is called "Swallow Butterfly Mornings", which is a cut-up of My Bloody Valentine's "Swallow" with Hope Sandoval & the Warm Inventions' (which is MBV's drummer) "Butterfly Mornings". On the page, it's a thing of gossamer beauty drawn out of pure noise cacophony. The poem couldn't be more different from the MBV song.

How do you know when a cut up poem is finished?

Good question. A cut-up has to have meaning in it, meaning that is different from the source material, and I instinctively know when that's the case. There has to be an energy there for the poem to work; it can't just be a pastiche. It has to be a unique emotional collage. Really good last lines are always crucial. They close the poem but open something up in the reader, hopefully.

Your previous collection were about the "play of light", this one is about sound. What plans do you have to cover the other senses, touch, taste and smell?

That would be an idea, wouldn't it? But I don't really have *a priori* plans – I tend to follow my nose and see what I come up with. As I say, my next project is to try my hand at some 'fractal' poems.

How do you choose which lyrics to cut up?

As I said, I chose the songs for the compatibility of their titles, genres, themes, but, in the case of the four "Songs" in *White Noise Machine*, I chose the two songs for their spiritual message. "Song: Hounds of Solsbury" is composed of lines cut from "Hounds of Love" by Kate Bush & "Solsbury Hill" by Peter Gabriel. Both those songs are about accepting change in one's life, a transformation to another state of being. The eagle and hounds in the songs are instruments/ metaphors for this change. "Song: Follow Heroes, Follow Me" is composed of lines cut from "Follow You, Follow Me" by Genesis & ""Heroes"" by David Bowie. Both are songs about wanting union, are invitations to stay together while acknowledging that that may not always be easy. "Song: Everybody, Don't Give Up" is composed of lines cut from "Everybody Hurts" by R.E.M. & "Don't Give Up" by Peter Gabriel. Both these famous songs are balms for the spirit, salves for the soul. They exhort us to defeat adversity, to cling on to hope. And, finally, "Song: Do You Realize You Are Everything?" is composed of lines cut from "Do You Realize?" by Flaming Lips & "You Are Everything" by R.E.M. Both of these intensely moving songs are a celebration of being alive, a tribute to the people in our lives and an acknowledgment of life's transience.

Do you have to ask for permission to use these lyrics?

I haven't put these cut-up poems into the public domain for profit. One publisher was interested in publishing them but withdrew because of copyright issues. As long as I'm not trying to profit from them, I think I'm ok.

I see. Great move. Have you ever used sources for cut-ups other than songs, such as advertising, prose, signage, official notices or newspaper articles?

Yes, prose. In *Terrace*, I published a cut-up of a quote from *The Lacemaker*, which is a French novel by Pascal Lainé. In *The Malvern Aviator*, I published a cento from *Wind, Sand & Stars* by Antoine Saint-Exupéry. And, most recently, in *Dream into Play*, I published an N+7 poem from *Criticism & Truth* by Roland Barthes. I'm a sucker for those French guys!

Do you ever combine cut up with original writing by yourself, or would this dilute the form?

No, they are two distinct disciplines for me. With cut-ups, I'm dealing with other people's words/lines, which takes the onus off me. It's kind of liberating. The process of my own work is a whole other story. A friend of mine once described the difference between writing fiction and non-fiction thusly: he said that writing non-fiction was about your enthusiasms whereas writing fiction was about your anxieties. For me, that's the same difference between the cut-ups and my own work.

Cut-ups seem to me to be very similar to collage artworks. What would you think about combining both disciplines?

Yes, as I've mentioned, cut-ups are very like collages. So, because they're so similar, I'm not sure what you mean about combining them.

Placing your cut ups onto collages.

No, I haven't considered that.

Once they have read *White Noise Machine*, what do you wish the reader to leave with?

Oh, I don't know. You can't direct readers. All you can do is write from the heart and soul and hope people connect in some way to what you write. Anything else is a bonus. But I believe that if you write with passion, your work stands a chance of finding passion within the reader. It's a transaction, but with no rules, no profits.

AN INTERVIEW WITH DAVID HARSENT

RS: When and why did you start writing poetry?

DH: I was eleven and on my way to Sunday School when I leaned over the first floor bannister at the post office building where my grandmother lived and worked, and where I had lived until I was nine, intending to slide down to the ground floor (something I often did), when I tipped over and fell the entire depth of the stairwell: about twenty-five feet. I still remember that fall, almost moment by moment. When the family doctor learned of this (he knew the geography of the building; he made a weekly call to my bed-ridden great-grandmother and my war-wounded father) he asked, 'Is he dead?'

Inexplicably, I was only concussed. After a couple of days in hospital I was taken back to the post office and (unnecessarily, I dare say) put to bed. It was decided, I don't know why, that my grandmother would take charge of my convalescence. Between the beef tea, the Lucozade, and the spaghetti hoops on toast, she went to the library to get me something to read – no TV, of course, and the radio was a piece of furniture the size of a dolls' house, anchored in the living room. Among the books she brought back was *A Bumper Book for Boys*, or some such tome. It contained accounts of derring-do – polar expeditions, jungle exploration, colonial triumphs, suicidal cavalry charges and hagiographical biographies of Baden Powell and other such grotesques. But between each account of a Thin Red Line or half-naked savages with nose-bones and a cooking-pot, some errant editor had slotted in a poem.

The poems held me. (I might say, *en passant*, that I really like the idea of a post-war radio as a dolls' house: in one room, a tiny Mrs, Dale writing her diary, in another Alvar Liddell reading the news, in a third, Dick Barton, Snowy and Jock, or Norman and Henry Bones, the boy detectives, bringing miscreants to justice.)

The poems held me, but I didn't know why. In part, it was the music, the four-beat/three-beat lines; but I was drawn to the narratives, which I only partly understood, of betrayal and revenge, of love and loss, of witchcraft and shape-shifting, of mischief and murder. The language was sometimes beyond me, but I found I could learn by example: the images were strong and the stories compelling, so meaning unraveled.

I asked my grandma to go back to the library and ask if there were any books that contained poems like these. She went. It's clear that the librarian knew her job, because grandma came back with Quiller Couch's *Oxford Book of Ballads*. The poems between the patriotic heroics were border ballads. Perhaps it was an act of sabotage by an editor with a likeable sense of humour. I read those poems day in, day out. I wrote 11-year old imitations of Tam Lin and the Demon Lover. I never returned the book to the library.

Who introduced you to poetry?

I had written poems and stories before this. When I was in primary school I wrote, as a classroom exercise, a story reworked (stolen) from a book I had at home, and a poem based on (stolen from) a book called *The Lord of the Rushie River*, the tale of a motherless girl whose father goes to sea and leaves his daughter in the care of a loathsome woman who treats the girl brutally and dresses her in rags. The girl's only friend is a swan, on whose back she rides as it flies. I was forbidden to read the book because it made me cry. I think I secretly wanted to be an ill-used orphan with a swan as my rescuer. I'd read – and had read to me – poems and stories, and I'd written stories and lines of my own, but I suppose it must have been Arthur Quiller Couch who stoked the fire.

How aware are and were you of the dominating presence of older poets traditional and contemporary?

One of the results of that fall was that I missed taking the 11-plus and, though I passed the 13-plus, went, at my father's insistence, not to the fine grammar school on offer, but to a Technical High School, to which I was wholly unsuited and which was, in any case, an appalling institution staffed by floggers, ignoramuses and thugs. Its academic record was farcical. It offered only technical subjects, save English and a recently adopted subject called the British Constitution, which I think was forced on it. No foreign language, no music, no history, no geography, but whole afternoons of metalwork technology and technical drawing. As a result, I left school at sixteen and didn't go to university. I was a fierce autodidact but, coming from a background which, despite my grandmother's middle-class origins and family connections, was working class in terms of housing (social), finance (minimal) and cultural appurtenances (scant). I had no mentor; my reading was based on guesswork and my choices unstructured. My plan was to read everything, and I tried to, but it was a bit like shuffling a deck of cards and turning either James Elroy Flecker or T.S.Eliot. I read randomly through the canon. Bit by bit, I more or less found the shape of things and formed opinions. I lived in the library and found that my job in a bookshop gave me the opportunity for systematic theft. My studies were also hampered by the fact that I was, in effect, a member of the working poor. I married early. As a teenage husband and father of a baby daughter, I was (we were) twice declared homeless. After that, we lived for six years in a two-up, two-down, cottage with no bathroom and an outdoor privy. My elder son was born in that place. I worked in the bookshop by day and wrote at night, through to the small hours. And I read in every spare moment. As a late-teenage and early-twenties aspirant, Modernism was my lynchpin.

What is your daily writing routine?

If I have something in hand, I work for most of the day. For a time, after the bookshop, and then a ten-year spell as a publisher, I funded my life by writing commercially, though I published poetry throughout those years and never really ever thought of myself as a screenwriter and/or thriller writer. When I was writing crime fiction or screenplays, I worked insane hours to get those tasks off my desk. There were always drafts of poems and open notebooks on my desk alongside plot-summaries and screenplay treatments. This is not to deride entertainment fiction or TV and film, it was just a matter of priorities. Truth to tell, it turned out I was pretty good at commercial writing and made a handsome living. I also taught in universities on and off. Most particularly, I spent a very enjoyable near-decade at the University of Roehampton where I was given enough leeway to be able to focus on poetry and writing for the opera stage not to have to watch the dawn come up as I signed off on another episode of 'Midsomer Murders'. And given my truncated educational record, I was (and am) pleased to have gained my professorship, my honorary doctorates and my fellowships. I've strayed from the subject…

What subjects motivate you to write?

My poems are fictions. I often trade off dream-images: that is to say, I adapt them; I put them to use. Of course, they're my dreams and I don't disown them, but the ensuing poem won't be autobiographical. I suppose it would be best to say I've never felt the urge to write from life. My purpose in poetry, more or less from the outset, has been to frame a narrative using a lyrical vocabulary. It wasn't ever a theoretical approach; I simply found myself doing it. The so-called Review Group, those poets most associated with Ian Hamilton's little magazine of that name, were said to (invariably) write short, interpersonal lyrics. The notion was that anything over eight lines was looked at disapprovingly. I was part of that group for a while, but my interest in the short lyric lay in how it might be the basis for an extended, though fragmented, narrative, one that would take the weight of progressive incident and event, and where the reader could trace a complex emotional pattern. 'A Dream Book' (*Fire Songs*) might be taken as a late example of this. I ought to add that my long-standing friendship with Ian Hamilton was another life-changing event.

Of course, there are, in my work, what might be called themes. When asked what do you write about? I used to say 'Sex and death'. The joke wore thin, though it was never really that much of a joke. John Burnside, in writing about my work, made mention of my focus on 'the human drama'. From the outset, interpersonal relationships have been a returning subject. So has that other dynamic of human conflict, war. I was born in what was called 'the worst year of the war'; people close to me were deeply affected by it; as a result, I was deeply affected by it. *Legion* is, perhaps, the most obvious response to that, but my versions of the poems Goran Simic wrote while besieged in Sarajevo, and of the poems Yannis Ritsos wrote while in prison or under house arrest during the Papadpoloulos dictatorship, were fed by the same impulse.

Another repeating theme is our brutal and soulless way with the natural world. The developing threat of the sixth great extinction has everything to do with our having lost touch with the subtle and complex mysteries of nature, that is to say with the creatures with whom we share the planet, with the creatures and with what grows and blooms and sustains. The European skies have lost 30 million birds since the 1950s. Britain's biodiversity record is atrocious; we are one of the most nature-depleted counties in the world. A million animal and plant species are close to extinction. That savage depletion is occurring in other countries year in, year out. Those who rule the planet, who govern, control and exploit it, seem to have no knowledge of the peril we're in. Or they simply can't conceive of – or tolerate, or allow – a world that is not for-profit. When I used the word soulless earlier, it was them I had in mind. What's needed is something akin to soul-retrieval. Capitalism stands in fierce opposition to that, as it always has.

Those themes find their way into the poem as it develops from that first nudge. They become part of the narrative; they illustrate it, direct it, become a narrative constituent. There's a better way of putting that, but to understand it better would be to court inhibition. I think of X.J. Kennedy's quatrain warning of the dangers involved in compositional scrutiny: *The goose that laid the golden egg / died looking up its crotch / to find out how it's sphincter worked. / Would you lay well? Don't watch.*

There are touchstone images in my poems: flight, birds in flight, a white bird on a blue (often white) sky, white on white, a white bed in a white room (black is erasure but white is effacement), a painting in which human figures are sensed only as a hidden weight in a white canvas (this appears only once, but informs much else), a 'white' book, water over stone, the hare: as interruptant and as the protagonist of a sequence, the Fool as interruptant, dreamwork/dreamlife, a house of women... These, and other, images, (also certain words and lines) will turn up from time to time in poems where they take on a different weight and energy, a different texture, a different narrative purpose.

I said, recently, of a sequence I'd written, that my characters carry the narrative. My concern with extended narrative (often fragmented) has very often led – logically enough – to sequences, some of them book-length. Apart from some poems from the early books – poems that might appear autobiographical, but are not – the only poems I've written that take a subject from the outset have been commissions (which I rarely accept). 'Bowland Beth' is probably the best (that is, most successful) example.

It's often said that my work is dark. I can see that it is. What most often provokes me is an image or a trigger-word or a part line. Where those opportunities come from is a mystery to me. The best I can say is that they crop up. Then lines accrue.

What is your work ethic?

I don't really know what that means. If it has something to do with motive, I'm not sure how that would (or could) apply. I simply take up the impulse to write when it occurs. Nabokov likened that feeling to a nudge. I recognise that: a hint, perhaps, but without subject; an uninterpretable whisper; or that I know something has (as it were) *entered*: something like a temperature change or a shadow falling. That apprehension will be quickly followed by an image or a word or half-line. It might, rarely, be a memory (it would never be an idea) though that will have been changed, blurred, in the recollecting and will almost at once develop as fiction -- memory being fiction anyway. Our histories, not least our emotional histories, are what we last remember.

How do the writers you read when you were young influence your work today?

I don't know; or, rather, I don't know if they do. I suppose those poems that moved or disturbed me will have left traces.

Whom of today's writers do you admire the most and why?

If I were to provide a list, I'd be certain to forget someone; or, perhaps, mention someone of whom I might come to think less well.

Why do you write, as opposed to doing anything else?

I assume you mean anything else in the arts. A significant part of my work, during the last thirty years, has been writing for the opera stage or for the concert hall. I've worked with several composers, but my collaborations with Harrison Birtwistle – four operas and as many song cycles over a period of thirty years or more – was a life-changing experience. The visual arts, painting in particular, have always been important to me. I wrote a long sequence that was loosely based on the relationship between Pierre Bonnard and the woman who called herself Marthe de Meligny. I gain emotionally and spiritually from painting, as with music, and always have done. I'm neither a composer nor a painter because I have no gift for either, but it's not a matter of choice or exclusion. I write because words are my means of interpreting the world. My vision is only achievable in (or through) poetry.

What would you say to someone who asked you 'How do you become a writer?'

Read.

You published your first collection, *A Violent Country*, with Oxford University Press in 1969 and went on to publish four more collections with OUP including *Mr Punch* (1984) and *News from the Front* (1993). Looking back on those early volumes, which parts of the work still stands the test of time in your view?

There is, I know, a notion that early collections are the work of one's apprenticeship, but I don't really hold with that. It can be the case, I suppose, that there's some sudden, sharp change of direction between early books and what is then seen as the poet's real purpose – affiliation with a movement or theory, or the (supposed) appearance of a mature style – but I think pursuing one's gift is most often a case of consolidating and developing subject, or finding that word-choice is becoming instinctive in the way it feeds lines. I think I set out my stall with those earlier books or, better perhaps, began a journey; I knew what steps I was taking but not where I was going. I still don't. It's been said of my work that I've never written two books that were alike. I suppose you could say that that's not quite true of

A Violent Country and *After Dark*, but that *Dreams of the Dead* was a departure, though it established my focus, I mean to say subject, which has remained pretty constant: what John Burnside referred to, in writing about *Loss*, as 'the human drama'. Even *Legion* held to that in its way (I have been told that a recent book by Andrew Duncan, on British poetry of the 1970s, had *Dreams of the Dead* as one of the key books of the '70s).

I see a constancy in my work. There's a line in *Loss* that I filched from a poem in *After Dark*. It's doing different work, but it's unchanged. That's a characteristic of my work: touchstone lines and images that reappear in the way that composers use themes or painters reference image. Their purpose, I think, is to provide evidence of continuing themes, but on each occasion, they are serving a different purpose. I don't summon them, they present themselves, and when they do, I almost never resist them. The really attentive close-reader would, I hope, go back to those touchstone words, phrases, images, narrative moments – that extended and continuing pattern – and look at the way they are central to specific passages and narratives, but also inform mood and purpose throughout. I ought to say that this particularly applies to my later work.

You moved to Faber in 1998 with *A Bird's Idea of Flight*. Several collections followed at regular intervals, including *Marriage* (2002), *Legion* (2005), *Fire Songs* (2014), *Salt* (2017) and *Loss* (2020). In each of these collections, I see a presiding structural conceit that drives the work. In *Flight*, for instance, it's (obviously) the circular journey; in *Marriage*, it's the 'mysteries of domesticity' as you call it; in *Legion*, it's the idea of the 'testimony' and in *Fire Songs* it's (again obviously) the 'song'. I think you're right to say that no two books of

yours are similar in form. Did the move affect you or your work in any way? Did these forms come more easily to you because you had so much work behind you by then?

There was an OUP contract on my desk for *A Bird's Idea of Flight* and the final version of the manuscript more or less ready to submit. Like many OUP poets, I'd been unhappy, for some time, with the senior management's apparent lack of commitment to the list. (Not, I hasten to add, the fault of the editor.) I think Hugo Williams had already jumped ship; I was more than ready to do the same. Of course, OUP – disgracefully – closed the list a year or so later: conclusive evidence of the way things were going.

I had begun my libretto for *Gawain* and was planning to make a final pass at *A Bird's Idea...* before sending it in. While I was working on the libretto, a weird thing happened. I interrupted myself, without knowing I was going to, when a scrap of verse came into my head. I stopped, scribbled those few words in my notebook, and went back to work. The lines were: *He was clean and gone / Long before the bus / Left the yard, Corpus / Christi writ thereon.* Where they came from: what prompted them, I can't remember; I'm not sure I ever knew; but obviously they'd come to mind for some reason. I can only suppose I'd read or seen or heard something that caused that errant compositional moment. As I continued with *Gawain*, interruptive lines kept cropping up. By the end of the day, I had...I can't remember, now...twenty or thirty such squibs in my notebook.

Over the next few days, while continuing to work on the libretto, I wrote more. In all there are sixty-three. It became evident to me, as they appeared, that I was writing the biography of a priest, who was tortured by uncertainty, temptation and the strictures of faith. Quite why was, and remains, a mystery to me. I was told once, by a bishop, that, having been brought up a Baptist, I would ('obviously') become a Catholic. My priest is Catholic. I thought, at first, that the squibs were a sort of exercise in comic extravagance. Then I saw that they were not. I published the sequence, privately, under the title *The Potted Priest* – 'potted', I suppose, because the poems were just a few lines each; only three hit the bottom of a very small page.

I sent the booklet to friends. One of them, Christopher Reid, responded very positively and suggested TPP would be 'everyone's book of the year'. At the time, Christopher was Faber's editor. He asked me, *en passant*, whether I happened to have a manuscript he might see. *A Bird's Idea of Flight* would have been something of a turning point for me whoever had published it; and a turning point it was, but not because it was taken on by Faber.

However, I think there might have been a sense of new freedom under Christopher's editorship. (I should add that my last book with OUP was *News from the Front*, and I still think well of that book.) Maybe the change itself, and the new energies to be found in Christopher's enthusiasm, the sheer professionalism of Faber, and being part of that list, gave a general sense of purpose and possibility that hadn't been evident at OUP. It was, definitely, a time of more intense writing: for years I wrote every day and seemed never without lines in my head and the beat of poetry in my ear. Having been asked about it, I recently went back to *Elsewhere*, the long poem that ends *Night*, my fourth Faber collection, and wondered how it was that I got up every day to write the next seven-line stanza of what became a poem of 749 lines.

I might say, *en passant*, that when Harrison Birtwistle and I were discussing a piece for Mark Padmore (who sang Orpheus in *The Corridor* and doubled as Jason and Aeson in *The Cure*), I asked Harry what he had in mind. He said, 'Perhaps a journey. You know, like Winterreise.' I mentioned that Elsewhere had been described, by one critic, as my Winterreise. Given that the Müller cycle, set by Schubert, is 380 lines and lasts 75 minutes, that notion wasn't pursued. The sequence I wrote, Harry set, and Mark sang was (after much to-ing and fro-ing and some misunderstanding) *Songs from the Same Earth* – 96 lines.

I think you're more or less right about what you call the structural conceits, the patterning, in the books you mention, apart perhaps from that in *Fire Songs*, the title of which, by the way, was suggested by Matthew Hollis, then my editor, who not only rescued the book from a somewhat desperate last minute attempt by me to find a title, but also persuaded sales-marketing to agree to a title change at a moment somewhat beyond the fifty-ninth minute of the eleventh hour. I thought the focus of the book would be the four Fire Songs that I saw as the spine of the book: that is its imperative, although there are poems in there that are no less crucial: *A Dream Book*, say, or *Songs from the Same Earth*. The latter was set as a song cycle by Harrison Birtwistle (was written for that) and considered by him to be among our most successful pieces.

The narrative of the four songs is not difficult to follow; it has an interpersonal thread which works in parallel with aspects of the climate crisis and historical accounts of conflict and barbarity. They form an inter-related and interdependent story. A man determines to destroy by fire everything he owns: the sequence starts with that. (I saw a TV show about Michael Landy's piece of performance art,

Break Down, in which he set about just that task.)

The first poem in the sequence, *Fire: a song for Mistress Askew* is an account of the torture, and death by burning, of Anne Askew, a Protestant martyr. She is cast as visionary and fire is a crucial factor throughout. Her prophetic utterance (given her by me) *It will be fire, it will be fire, it will be fire* is a significant and *propulsive* line that delivers energy, purpose and direction through the four poems. Evidence of the heat-death of the planet is present throughout: our indifference to the plundering of the planet, the consistent attack on the biosphere, now, in the later stages of the Anthropocene, the fact that we have lost touch with nature and its delicate mysteries of dependence and interdependence, the dominance of a brutal for-profit culture, persistent contempt for the sacred, and a refusal to understand that we are part of nature, informs the Fire Songs from start to finish.

I thought the suite of four Fire Songs would be the focus of the book and be given particular attention, but though the reviews overall were uniformly good, that didn't happen. Maybe the balance of the collection, or even its contents, might have needed to be differently managed to bring that about. My fault.

I don't think you need to worry about that. It seems to me that the four Fire Songs are the four pillars holding up the rest of the book. They are central to it. I'd like us to move on to your most recent collection, *Skin*, which was published by Faber in February 2024. I think it's a masterpiece. It's made up of 10 parts, each of which is discrete, but placed together, they pack one hell of an emotional punch. Some of them were published independently as pamphlets by some fantastic

small presses. Can you please talk about the genesis of these different parts and how they all fitted together?

As you say, some appeared before their inclusion in *Skin*: *Salt Moon* and *Nine* were both published by the wonderful Guillemot Press, *Of Certain Angels* came from Dare-Gale, a small publisher that has recently started a strong new list featuring contemporary poets, and Fine Press Poetry published a truly beautiful collectors' edition of a selection of poems from *Animals Silent in Darkness* under the title *A Clockwork Diorama*. So those were not conceived as part of a book-long series of sequences; nor, if it comes to that, were the other sequences in the book. However, given that much (I suppose most) of my work falls to sequences, it's not surprising that, eventually, a collection would consist of a series of sequences. This one has nine. The final, tenth, piece is a fractured narrative, whose parts can be described, I guess, as sequential.

Increasingly, my vision is best served, or so it seems, by a sustained narrative, though not (*Elsewhere* excepted) by long narrative poems, so my recent work has consisted most often of sequences and it seemed right that a new collection should contain them. Each piece, save for *Nine*, ends with an epigraph; someone reading through those epigraphs would, I think, get a pretty well-formed notion of what connects the sequences. (I don't want to characterize it: that's for others to do.) It's also the case that there are images, lines, key words, repetitions, that thread through my work: they all share – or, rather, came to share – aspects of the vision that (as with all artists) is my interpretation of the world: that is to say, the interiority that governs that interpretation. The way in which those images, lines, etc., can do different work in different places is (has become) part of the patterning in my work, and is a sort of visionary linkage. A short passage in the poem 'Room thirty-seven', from the sequence 'Hallways and Rooms' in *Skin,* is taken from a poem in my second collection, *After Dark,* fifty-one years and eleven books ago. The way in which that passage suddenly presented itself to me, and what it brings to the much later poem, came as a revelation.

I first saw the opportunities presented by a sustained, but broken, narrative during that time when I was around Ian Hamilton and the so-called New Review School. For me, those short, interpersonal poems only had weight and purpose as an interrogative sequence, where a sustained narrative developed aspects of 'the human drama'. It seemed to me that the characters involved needed more scope and space: that the reader deserved a better account of those little psychodramas and that this could be best done by, as it were, *turning the pages* to find different episodes from the drama in question. I have said before that 'my characters carry the narrative', this because I write little fictions: direct experience might sometimes colour certain lines, or provide detail, but I don't write autobiographically.

Ian published *Dreams of the Dead* in the New Review: not a sequence, a poem better described as episodic and, in terms of scope, unlike anything I'd written before. His belief in that sustained narrative gave me confidence. I went on from there. It's maybe worth noting that *Dreams of the Dead* was the title poem of only my third collection: this preoccupation goes back a long way.

The language in *Skin* is very dense. It's clear you have spent a great deal of time and effort in your word-choice and this care really stands out when one reads your work slowly. I've been reading your poetry pretty intensively for a number of

years now and what I've found is that it also works if one reads your work quite fast. There is thin ice between your work and the abyss beneath, so you have to skate fast over the words so that the ice doesn't break. I've found the same applies to the work of Geoffrey Hill, especially the later work. Why do you think this might this be the case?

No idea. All I can suggest is that because my sequences are fictions there's a narrative, though fragmented and (intentionally) incomplete, that might draw the eye. Reading my poems fast, as you describe, doesn't trouble me, but would were it not for your qualifying remark about word-choice and also reading slowly.

I'd like to turn your attention to *The Tanglewood Sonnets*. David, this is a staggering sequence of poems. I couldn't believe what I was reading when you sent them to me and I am very proud to be publishing them. We've talked about how alike they are to György Ligeti's *Études pour piano* in their stringency and brevity and for their impact. Can you please tell us a little bit about where these poems came from and how you formed them?

Tom Stoppard was once asked where he got his ideas from. He said, 'If I knew, I'd go there.' I recall Martin Amis being asked much the same question: where does it come from, not so much the reason to write – subject and compositional notion – but the impulse, and he quoted Nabokov responding to a similar question and likening the onset of a novel not to any formed idea, but to something akin to a nudge, an alertness. I would say, an emotional awakening. I know there are poets who decide on (arrive at) a subject and make a plan, not least, I think, when they have an extended piece in view -- a sequence, perhaps. I can see how that works and I don't deride it, but with me it's the nudge.

My younger son, Barnaby, when he was small, once asked me: 'Your poetry – do you just make it up as you go along?' I admitted that, yes, that was pretty much what I did. What tends to happen (and I don't want to think too closely about it) is that lines and images arrive, dependent on each other, and I make sketches, and things start to take shape. Obviously, as I progress, as the poem – more often a sequence – progresses, things become richer, more opportunities present themselves, the narrative becomes self-sustaining, characters advance that narrative – an emotional development – and music and word-choice provoke new opportunities. (I don't suppose this is unique to me.) Sometimes, as I've mentioned, certain touchstone images and lines fall in, or 'crop up' might be more accurate, and enrich the mix with echoes of, or references to, earlier work, that shed light on the work in hand. (I think that might be unique to me.) So, the compositional me is focused on the lines as I write, but the instinctual me is, at the same time, reaching out.

I've said that some of my work (*Elsewhere* is an example) seems to get written – or, at least, get underway – in a sort of fever-dream. My joke title for the Fire Songs poems (that set of poems, not the collection) was 'Red Mist'. I can feel that I'm not giving a very accurate account of this, but that's not surprising, perhaps, since I'm trying to describe not just something as abstract as a nudge and the way that nudge develops, but a nudge, and a development, both personal and particular.

I mentioned, earlier, the poetry identified with the group that was connected to the Review and the New Review: that it was notable for its interpersonal content and its brevity. My particular interest, also mentioned earlier, but worth repeating here, since it throws light on the *Tanglewood* poems, was in the way that a series of short poems might connect to make a discernable narrative: a chain-narrative, if you like, 'beads on a string' was one reviewer's description. I have pursued that notion: an extended narrative given in brief (though, as things have gone on, less brief) scenes from a drama that probably starts *in medias res* and might draw to a close but have no obvious conclusion. (This pattern isn't invariable; I have written single-subject poems; but it's usual.)

The Tanglewood Sonnets is such a narrative. It can, I think, be read as a novel, if the reader is prepared to use its images, its episodes, its musical hints, and its word-choice, as a means to gaining its dramatic shape and narrative drift; that is, the reader might also make it up as he/she goes along. However, that structure isn't what I had in mind from the outset. I just felt the nudge and waited and then began to write. I ought to say, perhaps, that these are sonnets more or less by accident: that form wasn't what I'd planned. Starting to fashion lines for the first poem, I wrote a couplet, then embellished the next two lines with a third, and so on. It was when I began the quintain that I saw what was going on, and went with what I seemed to have fallen in to. They're not sonnets, of course, they're fourteen-liners, but I'm happy to adopt the loose description that is current. As it happens, instinct served me well. Fourteen (as it turned out) fourteen-liners was what the narrative stretch wanted.

Thank you for that very comprehensive and illuminating description of your process. To me, it seems as if these poems are carved on air. They come from nowhere with such power. Truly remarkable. What's in store for you in the future? Have

you felt the nudge of any new work?

I never stop working. I work from dreams, or out of dreams, and my notebook gets used pretty much every day. There was a short pause after *Of Certain Angels*, the Guillemot edition of *Nine,* and Bloodaxe bringing out *A Broken Man in Flower* – my versions of the poems Yannis Ritsos wrote while in prison camps and under house arrest during the Papadopoulos junta during the mid sixties and early seventies. Not long before that, Guillemot published *Salt Moon*, a collaboration with my elder son, his photographs, my poems; then, a bit later, Faber published *Skin*, my fourteenth collection (some of the limited edition poems went into that). Maybe, given that output, a break was inevitable, but it made me uneasy. If I'm not writing, I don't know what I'm for.

When Harrison Birtwistle died in 2022 a significant part of my compositional life was curtailed. Harry and I had collaborated, on and off, for more than thirty years. The moment when he cold-called me, to ask whether I'd consider writing an opera with him, changed my life. The opera was *Gawain.* It opened at the Royal Opera House. That piece, our subsequent work for the opera stage, plus song cycles and solo pieces, were (and still are) performed worldwide. When he died, we were talking about (and I was making notes and sketches for) a Glyndebourne commission that will now never happen.

After that cold call, Harry became a close friend, and our work together was an indivisible part of my life. There is no easy way for me to characterize its importance to, and influence on, my creative thinking. Harry's was the most interesting mind I have ever met. His way of encountering the world through his art was deep, wholly unique, always revelatory; being close to that, being part of it, was exhilarating. I miss him and I mourn him, and I thank the gods (of whom, in *The Minotaur*, I say *[they] look down and laugh*) for bringing us together.

I hope, though, that my life in music will continue. I'm currently talking about new pieces with three very gifted composers, all of whom I've collaborated with on work performed at major venues, and we're eager to start work. We need commissions, of course, and are hopeful, despite the fact that the arts in this country have been systematically trashed and deliberately defunded over the past decade or more. That aside, I've written fairly seamlessly since I moved to Surrey from London two and a half years ago. Before we found somewhere to buy we rented and I found myself, pretty much by accident, living on the Pilgrim's Way, close to Gunpowder Mills, then in a house called Tanglewood, now in Wonersh, (middle English for 'crooked field') near Blackheath, names all of which prompted lines, though lines very far from the 'poems of place' that those titles might suggest. At present, I'm working on a poem called *The Dance of the White Spider*. The white spider has been cropping up, lately, as a touchstone image. You'll be unsurprised to learn that I've no idea why or how that little critter appeared on the page; nor do I yet know quite what it wants of me.

ACKNOWLEDGEMENTS

Huge thanks to Aaron Kent and his team at Broken Sleep Books for publishing this book. I am very grateful.

For originally commissioning/publishing some of these pieces, or versions of these pieces, and for comments and support, my thanks go to Victoria Best, Blandine & Paul @ Black Herald Press, Paul Brookes, Nuzhat Bukhari, David Cooke, Greg Freeman @ WriteOutLoud, Maria Fusco, Andrew Gallix @ 3:AM magazine, David Harsent, Alan Humm, James McKenzie, Pablo's Eye & Push @ Electronic Sound magazine.

Thanks to Phil Clark and Jason Watkins for their help with "'How does that old song go?' – *Deserter's Songs* at 25."

Thanks to Abby Wilkinson for the image in "Proust's 'cross-hatching of instants'".

My love and gratitude always to J.

LAY OUT YOUR UNREST